COOKING WITH

AMAR'E

COOKING WITH

AMAR'E

100

easy recipes
for pros
and rookies
in the kitchen

AMAR'E STOUDEMIRE
AND CHEF MAXCEL HARDY III

WITH ROSEMARY BLACK

itbooks

AN IMPRINT OF HARPERCOLLINS PUBLISHERS

*it*books

COOKING WITH AMAR'E. Copyright © 2014 by Amar'e Stoudemire and Maxcel Hardy III. All rights reserved.
Printed in the United States of America. No part of this book may be used or reproduced in any manner
whatsoever without written permission except in the case of brief quotations embodied in critical articles
and reviews. For information address HarperCollins Publishers, 195 Broadway, New York, NY 10007.

HarperCollins books may be purchased for educational, business, or sales promotional use. For
information please e-mail the Special Markets Department at SPsales@harpercollins.com.

All photographs © by Am Media Group

FIRST EDITION

Designed by Lorie Pagnozzi

Library of Congress Cataloging-in-Publication Data has been applied for.

ISBN 978-0-06-232518-1

14   15   16   17   18   ID6/QWT   10 9 8 7 6 5 4 3 2 1

FROM AMAR'E:

For my wife and children, I hope this book can be a light to all young fathers to become better cooks for their families.

FROM MAX:

With love and gratitude I dedicate this book to:

My mother, Lavern Arnett, for loving me, teaching me good values, and instilling religion in my life that has gotten me this far.

My father, Maxcel Hardy, Jr., for showing me what it means to be a family man, father, and friend.

My daughter, Tenara Demi Hardy, for keeping Daddy grounded and giving me a reason to work hard every day.

Cheryl Hardy, thanks for helping to raise me and for being an amazing support system.

Chef Richard Roberts (Uncle Rich) . . . for guiding me through this culinary journey, and helping me transition to become a man and a strong father.

Ellen Sadove Renck, for believing in me and loving me unconditionally, and helping to bring Chef Max Miami to life.

Chef Edward Burjaski for introducing me to Culinary Arts and helping me figure out that cooking is my true passion. Thanks for preparing me for Johnson & Wales.

CONTENTS

We first met five years ago in Miami. At the time Max was a rising culinary star and Amar'e was a pro ball player in need of someone to cater a dinner party he was having—that very night. Max, a genius in the kitchen even under great pressure, whipped up a lavish meal on short notice and the rest is history. Within a year, our working arrangement was set. But as our friendship blossomed, our relationship morphed from chef and client to teacher and student. The kitchen became a classroom where the questions flowed: How do you use this knife? How do you make salsa from scratch? What vegetarian dishes could you make for the kids that they would actually enjoy eating? Through impromptu cooking lessons, lessons that over time became more formalized and complex, Amar'e gained confidence and skills in the kitchen. We've come a long way from that dinner party back in Miami. These days, Amar'e not only hosts but also cooks for his guests. But the real joy of cooking comes when preparing a healthy and tasty meal the kids love.

This book expands upon these informal cooking lessons and is meant to help you find your stride in the kitchen by teaching you the important cooking techniques and basic ingredients every cook should become familiar with. We have given you a wide range of recipes that are tailored to every level of expertise, from beginner to pro. And we've provided you with tips and ideas to streamline your cooking.

Before you tie on an apron, take a few minutes to read through the Essentials chapter, where you'll learn about ingredients, techniques, and tools, and get some basic recipes. Then, as you move on through the rest of the recipes, you'll find each one labeled according to the level of difficulty. Easy recipes are marked Layup, those that can be made by anyone who has been cooking for a while are called Jump Shot, and the most challenging recipes are labeled Slam Dunk.

New to the kitchen? Cook up some of the Layup dishes, the same ones Amar'e got started with, until you feel more comfortable at the stove. Before you know it, you'll have mastered the basics and be ready to impress your family and friends with the more complex dishes.

Each recipe also contains a headnote that is written with you in mind. These notes may highlight a serving suggestion, a tip on storage, guidance on how to execute the directions, or advice on how to streamline the preparation. You'll also find instructional sidebars scattered throughout the book—these are to assist you as you cook and to give you confidence (and some swag!) as you whip up break-fasts and brunches, lunches and snacks, and dinners to wow your family and friends.

Finally, a couple of practical notes: When a recipe calls for eggs, they should be large unless otherwise specified. Flour is always all-purpose unbleached flour. When a recipe calls for salt, it should be kosher salt, and when it calls for pepper, it should be freshly ground. Usually, the instructions for seasoning with salt and pepper are "to taste." It makes sense to add just a little, then taste, and then add a little more as needed. Cooking is all about flexibility, trying out new tastes, and realizing that you can and should personalize these recipes until they taste just the way you want them to.

We hope this book will be a starting point for you to enhance your kitchen skills, that it will help you feel creative and comfortable around the stove, and that the food you prepare for your family and friends will always be full of love.

Amar'e and Max

AMAR'E

I cook like I play basketball: I want to be the best that I can be at both. I am competitive when I'm on the court, and it's easy for me to get competitive about cooking, too. I want everything I make to be perfect. But it took me some time to get where I am today in the kitchen. I have lived and breathed basketball for as long as I can remember. But cooking didn't interest me until a couple of years ago. When I was growing up, I was a tall, skinny kid with a lot to do, and so back then, I grabbed food just to fill me up. I didn't pay that much attention to what I was eating or how it was prepared. When I was just starting out in the NBA at age nineteen, I would make quick meals for myself if I had to, but they were nothing fancy.

It wasn't until I became a dad that I began to take more of an interest in food. As a father, I wanted the very best for my children, and that included wanting them to eat well. That didn't mean I ate nutritiously. Like most parents, I was probably better at making sure my kids ate a well-balanced diet than I was at eating one myself.

Then Chef Max came to cook for us, and I really started to appreciate good food. Max has been such an inspiration to all of us. He creates amazing recipes that taste great and are filling and

1

healthy. He's shown me how even a very simple food, like a potato, can be cut into wedges and baked to make a tasty snack or side dish. Max got me so interested in healthy cooking that I asked him to show me how to cook. In the two years that he has been teaching me, I have come a long way. I knew I had improved when I didn't even need to call on Max to cook up something for a dinner party I was hosting. I had it covered. But I'll admit that he continues to teach me a lot every time we share a kitchen together.

I like simple yet flavorful foods, like braised kale, stewed okra, and baked sweet potato "fries." I love making my vegetarian chili, though I had never even heard of ground tofu until I met Max. When I eat food like this, I don't miss the junk food.

Of course, there are some not-so-healthy foods that have been hard to give up. My weaknesses? Fried chicken, mac and cheese, cheeseburgers, and ice cream. Now I just eat less of them, and I keep them in my repertoire for special occasions.

Barbecued ribs, steak, and fried fish with grits all taste even better now that I know how to make them myself. These dishes give me energy on the court, and they have staying power.

As Max's student in the kitchen, I learned a lot. From chopping to sautéing and everything in between. He taught me how to make slam dunk meals for myself and my family. And I am excited to share so many of these wonderful recipes and tips with you in the following pages. Like basketball and family, food has become another passion in my life, and I hope this book inspires you to get more familiar with what you put on your plate every day.

MAX

As Amar'e Stoudemire's personal chef, I have the best job in the world, combining my two great loves: cooking and basketball. I learned to cook in the culinary arts program in my local high school. When the chef in charge of the school's culinary program asked me if I wanted to cater some events with him for school functions, I helped him out. Cooking was something I was good at and I liked.

At the same time, I was a shooting guard on my high school basketball team and I wanted to be an NBA star.

Luckily, I had a plan B: becoming a chef. My uncle is a chef, and many members of my family are amazing cooks. I enrolled in Johnson & Wales University in Miami on a full basketball and culinary scholarship, and graduated at the top of my class. I was lucky enough to get a spot as an executive chef before I turned twenty-one. Between being a chef and cooking for my celebrity

clients, I stayed busy. My fusion cuisine—a blend of American, French, Asian, and Caribbean—attracted hip-hop artists, actors, professional athletes, and dignitaries.

I first met Amar'e five years ago when he got in touch to see if I could prepare a dinner party for him one weekend. I had just finished cooking for a client and was packing up to go home. Amar'e wanted me to cook for him that night, as in, right now!

It was almost midnight, but I made it happen. I had some unused ingredients from the meal I'd just cooked for my client. After doing a little shopping, I whipped up a grand feast—grilled lobster tails, steaks, Yukon Gold potato–garlic mash, and chocolate soufflé. From that point on, Amar'e and I stayed in contact off and on. Two years later, Amar'e called to invite me to come cook for him in Los Angeles during the week he was scouting a different team to get traded to. I cooked for him for about a week and a half and at the end of it, I got some exciting news: Amar'e wanted me to be his personal chef. Four months later, I moved to New York. I've been Chef Max to the Stoudemire family ever since.

In the beginning, my job was challenging. When I first started to cook for Amar'e, he was a meat-and-potatoes kind of guy. But I gradually saw his palate change as I started serving some dishes he'd never tasted, like Almond-Crusted Sole with Ginger Lime Beurre Blanc and my killer Vegetarian Chili.

Cooking for Amar'e is a tall order (no pun intended). Amar'e, whose mother is Jewish, likes me to buy kosher food in keeping with his Hebrew background, although he doesn't keep strictly kosher. Sometimes, he wants to eat only vegetarian food for weeks or months at a time. He says that avoiding foods made with animal products makes him feel better and gives him more energy. He needs to consume around 6,000 calories a day during basketball season, and it's important that he eat energizing, balanced meals. During the season, he practices for hours every day and has pretty intense caloric needs. Every dish needs to count. They can't just contain empty calories.

Keeping pace with Amar'e's nutritional demands keeps me a busy man. I spend hours every day just shopping for food before I even start cooking. But I love it. I have incredible flexibility, and free rein to create different dishes for Amar'e and his family. And besides the fact that I have the best job in the world, I'm happy because I get to hang out with Amar'e's team.

Over time, the friendship Amar'e and I developed has deepened. I wouldn't say he is a food guru, but he is much more interested in eating well and about a year ago, he expressed an interest in learning to cook. In my role as his cooking teacher, I've happily watched him become very comfortable at the stove. Amar'e has made so much progress as a chef since we started hanging out together in the kitchen. I'm looking forward to helping you learn the same basic techniques and wonderful dishes I've shared with him, and I appreciate the opportunity to share my expertise and my recipes with you.

5

THE ESSENTIALS

“AMAR'E

The first thing that Chef Max taught me about cooking is that before you even start, it's important to have all the ingredients you need all set and ready to go. This is called your *mise en place* (a French term) and it really makes a lot of sense. Before I realized how crucial it is to check and double-check that all you need to make a particular dish is close at hand, cooking was much harder.

The other piece of great advice that I got from Max is to read your recipe all the way through before you proceed. It's easy to be impatient, because you want to see delicious results, but in order to make a winning dish that will score points with your family and friends, it's important to take the time to read the recipe from start to finish.

What is not so important, when it comes to being a good cook, is the size of your kitchen. My family and I live in an apartment in New York City, with a kitchen that can barely fit two grown people into it—especially when one of them is nearly seven feet tall. Yet all the great cooking that happens in that small space is nothing short of amazing. That's because what it lacks in size, our kitchen makes up for in efficiency. Packed into the tight space are all the essential tools and cookware that Chef Max needs to turn out the breakfasts, lunches, snacks, and dinners that wow my family every day.

The kitchen is outfitted with as much cookware as we need for a family of six, but the supply is not overabundant. I think it's important to have the tools you need but not so much stuff that the room begins to seem cluttered. If you drink a lot of smoothies, you should invest in a good blender, and if you love ice cream as much as I do, there has to be room in your kitchen for an electric ice cream maker. But that doesn't mean you need to go out and buy a special rotisserie for grilling a turkey or a fryer that makes minidoughnuts. Keep things simple, buy the best knives, skillets, and saucepans that you can afford, and make sure your kitchen is a happy, warm gathering place.

Besides being warm and efficient, our kitchen is just a nice place to spend time. Just outside it, on our wrap-around terrace, fresh figs thrive, fresh herbs grow in

8

pots, ready to be snipped and used to flavor vegetables, grains, and meats, and a massive gas grill stands at the ready. The party inside tends to spread out to this terrace in the warm weather, since the kitchen's not large enough for guests to hang out. But even though the kitchen is small and we have a lot of company to entertain, these days I like being there to help get the food ready. It's all the party I need.

MAX 99

Before you start cooking, it is important to have a knowledge and understanding of the different ingredients you will be using. Learning about the various vegetables and cuts of meat is important, as is understanding cooking terminology and techniques, and developing basic knife skills. I teach these culinary techniques and concepts to the high school students I mentor in the Opportunity Charter School in Harlem in New York City, and I want you to master them, too. So before you get cooking, here's some information to get you started, along with the basic recipes that truly are the foundations for any good cook.

FOUL PLAY

Now that I've gotten some one-on-one cooking
lessons from a world-class chef, my confidence
in the kitchen is finally at a level where I'm
comfortable making a cozy family supper for
six or a hearty team dinner for twenty.

But many scorched soups and stews, botched roasts and rib eyes, and inedible biscuits and burritos happened before I reached the point where I could grill steaks or simmer chili without the smoke detector's wails sending everyone scurrying out of the kitchen.

Most of my kitchen mishaps have centered around the stove. When I was first learning to cook, I constantly put too much olive oil in a pan after I set it on the burner. I'd switch the flame to high and put in the food which, of course, cooked a lot faster than I anticipated. Next thing I knew, the smoke detector was going off again. Since then I've definitely learned to lighten my hand where the olive oil bottle is concerned. My early attempts to make grilled cheese sandwiches were also an epic fail. I used to turn up the flame too high, thus burning the bread to the point where I had to scrape black ashes off the bread.

The barbecue grill was another scene of frequent mealtime disasters. Blackened hot dogs come to mind when I think of the time I tried to cook them for the kids. I would put the hot dogs on the charcoal grill before the coals were hot. The result was that the smoke from the charcoal caused the dogs to smell and taste like lighter fluid. Not one of my finer moments as a chef!

One of the very first things Max taught me about cooking was how to use a chef's knife. This is a very important kitchen technique to master because you use a knife for just about everything. But as much as I wanted to mince, dice, and chop like an expert, my hands got in the way. They're so big that it took me a few tries to find my grip on the knife. I would say that mastering knife skills was a real challenge for me.

But gradually the cooking mishaps stopped occurring so frequently. And slowly but surely, my friends and family realized that I had developed some smooth kitchen moves and started to take my cooking seriously. I'm happy and proud to put a meal I've made on the table, to see how delicious it looks, and to watch everyone enjoy it.

PRODUCE PRIMER:
10 OF OUR FAVORITES

Learning to incorporate a wide variety of fruits and vegetables into daily meals not only makes every dish more interesting and delicious, but it also makes for healthier eating, since produce is filled with so many health-boosting antioxidants. Fruits and vegetables have so much going for them, and they come in such a colorful, flavorful assortment, that it's fun to break out of the rut of eating only the same old reliable few, and try something new. Here are a few colorful, not so common, varieties worth sampling.

COLLARD GREENS: Are very popular in Southern cooking, have a mild flavor, and can be stored longer than other types of greens. In a sealed plastic bag, the unwashed leaves will keep for up to five days in the refrigerator.

KALE: Kale is so trendy these days that it seems to be almost omnipresent in high-end restaurants, cafés, and fancy takeout shops. But before it was so fashionable, kale was a relatively humble cruciferous vegetable that was often stewed or braised. When you cook kale, remove the tough center stem. Use kale within a couple of days after you buy it or the leaves will grow limp and the flavor quite strong.

MANGOES: Are juicy, fragrant, and a sweet addition to salads, salsas, and smoothies. That said, they are a little more challenging to prepare than certain other fruits. Once you peel away the tough green skin, you will still need to deal with the stubborn, flat pit in the center. Either cut slices of mango with a sharp knife, simply avoiding the center pit, or make a series of cuts in both directions on the mango and then dice the mango.

OKRA: Sold fresh and frozen, okra develops a viscous texture once it is cooked, making it a natural to thicken a variety of stews and gumbos. The pods should be small (under 4 inches), firm, and unblemished. You can store okra for up to three days in the refrigerator, in a plastic bag.

PARSNIPS: Parsnips, which resemble long white carrots, should always be cooked, as they will become sweeter. Look for parsnips that are evenly col-

13

ored and no more than 10 inches long, as the larger ones tend to have less flavor and even some bitterness. Be sure to scrub them, peel them, and cut off both ends.

PIGEON PEAS: This teeny legume, native to Africa, is popular in Latin American cooking and often combined with rice for a filling side dish. Usually dried and split, they also can be found canned, fresh, and frozen.

POTATOES: You'll want to choose a potato based on what you plan to do with it. Russets, large and rough-skinned potatoes (Idahos are a type of russet), make the most wonderful French fries, and they also are great for baking whole. Waxy potatoes, which are smooth-skinned and are either white or red, are great for sautéing or in dishes where it is important that they hold their shape. For mashed potatoes, avoid waxy potatoes and instead choose Yukon Gold potatoes. If you are making French fries, cut the potatoes into wedges that are about $1/2$-inch thick. For thinner "shoestring" fries, cut the potatoes into strips that are about $1/4$-inch thick.

RUTABAGAS: Like turnips and parsnips, rutabagas are delicious boiled and mashed, or added to stews and soups. Look for rutabagas that are on the small side—three to five inches is the perfect size—since these will be the sweetest. Choose rutabagas that feel heavy for their size and are free of blemishes and soft spots.

SWEET POTATOES: While there are many varieties, one of the most common is the dark sweet potato, which has a thicker skin and darker flesh than the pale yellow sweet potato. The peak season for sweet potatoes is winter. Try to find those that are small to medium, with smooth skins, and store them in a cool, dark place. If stored in a cool, dark, dry place, they will keep for up to three weeks. Sweet potatoes are not the same thing as yams, which are brown-skinned and have a yellow or white flesh.

TURNIPS: Turnips are a versatile root vegetable that can be added to soups and stews, diced raw and put into salads, or boiled. Ideally, turnips will still have a few greens attached when you buy them. It's fine to buy them even if the greens are not attached, but always choose small ones, and look for turnips that are heavy for their size.

SOME USEFUL COOKING TERMS

If you're preparing to follow a recipe but can't decipher some of the ingredients or directions, your time in the kitchen is going to be like a losing game: a frustrating experience that you don't want to repeat. To ensure that every dish you make is a winner and to make you the happiest cook in the kitchen, here are ten cooking terms that are used often throughout this book. Read on to know the difference between mincing and chopping, and what it means to sear versus sauté.

BRAISE: To cook a food by first browning it in oil or another fat and then adding a small amount of liquid, covering it, and simmering it over low heat until tender and flavorful. It's typical to cook meat and vegetables using this method.

CARAMELIZE: To heat sugar until it becomes a clear syrup ranging from golden to brown. Often, it's done under the oven broiler or with a little hand-held kitchen torch.

CHIFFONADE: This is an ideal way to prepare tender herbs like basil and sage, since chopping these can cause them to bruise and darken. Roll up a stack of four leaves lengthwise, jelly roll–style, and slice across the roll into very thin slices, using a very sharp knife.

DICE: To cut food into $\frac{1}{8}$- to $\frac{1}{4}$-inch pieces; technically, diced food is cut smaller than cubed food.

FOLD: This technique is used when you want to combine a lighter mixture (like beaten egg whites or whipped cream) with a heavier mixture (such as a batter). The lighter mixture is piled on top of the heavier one and then a spatula repeatedly slices down through both mixtures on one side of the bowl and then up the other side, until the mixtures are combined.

HERBES DE PROVENCE: An assortment of dried herbs that usually has basil, marjoram, rosemary, summer savory, and thyme, along with certain others. It is used to flavor soups, stews, and dips.

MINCE: To cut food into teensy pieces—when a food is minced, it's in teenier pieces than when it's chopped or diced.

MISE EN PLACE: In French, this means having all your ingredients together in one place before starting to cook.

SAUTÉ: The act of cooking food in a large, shallow pan in a small amount of oil or butter over fairly high heat. This method works well for chicken cutlets and thin steaks, but not so well with larger steaks.

SEAR: Very little or no butter is used in this cooking method, which is done in a pan over high heat and which creates an appealing crust on the surface of meat or fish.

SOME HELPFUL HOW-TOS

On the court or at the stove, to be at the top of your game means knowing how to execute a variety of plays, to polish each and every technique, and to put your own signature style into everything you do. You may never make basketball your profession, but that doesn't mean you can't make cooking your avocation—and be the best at it that you can be. In this glossary of how-tos, you'll get some extra coaching on how to mince, grate, and slice like a professional chef.

HOW TO MAKE THE ULTIMATE BURGER: Form your burgers with a light touch, never compressing the meat with your hands, or you'll be left with a dense, dry burger. Make a tiny indentation with your thumb right in the center of the burger so it will stay flat in the skillet.

HOW TO PREPARE LEEKS: Remove the tough stem ends from the leeks and soak the leeks in a large bowl of cold water for about half an hour to remove any impurities. Using a chef's knife, slice each leek lengthwise into thin strips. Next, cut the leeks crosswise so that you are left with diced leek.

HOW TO PREPARE FRESH GINGER: Cut off the amount you want to use and peel off the skin with a sharp knife. Grate the ginger on the fine side of a box grater or place it on the work surface and chop it with a sharp chef's knife.

HOW TO PREPARE BERRIES: Store berries in the refrigerator but don't wash them until you're ready to use them. Run water over the berries in a colander and place them on a plate lined with paper towels to dry. Refrigerate until serving time.

HOW TO PREPARE FRESH CORN: Pull off the husks and any of the silk that is attached to the kernels. Drop the ears into a large pot of boiling water, reduce the heat, and cook for about 7 minutes. To grill corn, remove the husks from the corn, place the ears of corn on a grill set on medium-low, and grill for about 15 minutes, turning occasionally, or until lightly browned on all sides.

HOW TO PREPARE FENNEL: Trim the stalks from the fennel and pull off and discard the tough outer layers of the bulb. Remove the core with a sharp knife. Roughly chop the fennel, using a chef's knife.

HOW TO SEED A TOMATO: The easiest way to do this is to cut the tomato in half (basically across the equator) and squeeze each half to get out the seeds. Discard the seeds and liquid.

HOW TO DICE A TOMATO: Remove the core of the tomato with a small, serrated sharp knife. Cut the tomato in half from stem to blossom end. Place the tomato, cut side down, on a cutting board. Make thin parallel slices, using a sharp knife, in each half, cutting through all the way. Rotate the tomato slightly and make thin parallel slices going in the opposite direction. Chop the tomato into $1/4$-inch dice. Depending upon whether you want the tomatoes to retain their liquid, you may want to use as is or place them into a colander so the liquid will drain off.

HOW TO CHOP SHALLOTS: Place the shallots on a cutting board. Place the side of the chef's knife blade on top of each, and strike it lightly to break the skin. Peel off the skin. Next, place the shallots on a cutting board and slice them into strips. Place all the strips in the center of the cutting board and rock the chef's knife back and forth

over the pile, keeping one hand on the handle of the blade and the other steadying the blade, with your fingers spread out over the blade so that your hand is parallel to the cutting board.

HOW TO PREPARE MUSHROOMS: Before using mushrooms, place them into a large bowl of cold water and set them aside for 5 minutes. Swirl them around the water for a few seconds, then drain into a colander. Store mushrooms in the refrigerator in a paper bag rather than a plastic bag, which will make them spoil more quickly. For sautéed mushrooms, trim away the stem end and slice each mushroom into thick slices. Since mushrooms hold a lot of water, sauté them a few at a time in very hot oil so they won't release a lot of water into the pan and end up steamed rather than sautéed.

HOW TO CHOP AN ONION: Cut the onion in half lengthwise and peel the skin back to the root. Leave the root intact, but cut off the very top of each onion half. Place the onion, cut side down, on a cutting board. Slice the onion several times, first lengthwise and then widthwise, going nearly all the way but not quite through. Then cut across the onion right up to the root. For finer pieces, just make the cuts closer together.

HOW TO SLICE AN ONION: Cut the onion in half lengthwise and peel the skin back to the root. Leave the root intact but cut off the very top of each onion half. Place one onion half, cut side down, on a cutting board. Working your way from the tip of the onion to the root, make neat, even slices, then cut off the root.

HOW TO MINCE GARLIC: Using your hands, remove the number of cloves that you will need from the garlic bulb. Place one on a cutting board. With a large chef's knife, press the clove firmly to almost flatten it. It will feel like you are smashing the clove, but that's okay. The papery skin is now loose enough that you can peel it. Repeat this with the remaining cloves. Next, place the cloves on a cutting board and slice them into strips. Place all the strips in the center of the cutting board and rock the chef's knife back and forth over the pile, keeping one hand on the handle of the blade and the other steadying the blade, with your fingers spread out over the blade so that your hand is parallel to the cutting board.

ESSENTIAL KITCHEN EQUIPMENT

If you are just starting out in the kitchen, the array of utensils, cookware, gadgets, and gizmos sold in department stores, housewares shops, and online can be quite bewildering. Even if you've been cooking for awhile, you probably find yourself wondering whether you need more than what you already own. Here is a list of the most indispensable cookware and kitchen tools, the ones you will find yourself keeping close at hand and using over and over.

DUTCH OVEN: For stews and braised dishes, this two-handled, ovenproof vessel is perfect. It performs many of the same functions as a sauté pan and a large saucepan in that you can brown foods in it first and then add meat and a liquid such as stock, cover it, and simmer until the meat is tender. Look for one that holds around 5 quarts and preferably is made of enameled cast iron or stainless steel with an aluminum core.

GRILL PAN: Want to get the taste of barbecued steaks, burgers, and chicken even when the weather is not conducive to cooking outside? Invest in one of these handy pans, which have a ridged surface that allows fat or cooking liquid to drain off and also makes those coveted grill marks that you get when you cook on a grill outside.

SAUTÉ PAN: A 10-inch pan, which has sloped sides, is perfect for cooking vegetables, browning chops and steaks, and making omelets. Since aluminum is an excellent heat conductor, try to find one that has an aluminum core.

SAUCEPAN: Having two of these straight-sided pots, preferably a 2-quart and a 4-quart size, will make your life easier when it comes to heating up soups, cooking vegetables, making sauces, and cooking rice, quinoa, and couscous. Stainless steel is ideal for a saucepan. Be sure they come with a lid, and consider investing in a steamer insert for one of them so that you can easily steam fresh vegetables or even seafood.

STOCKPOT: Invest in an 8- or 10-quart stockpot and you will use it for everything from making soups and stocks to pasta and even corn on the cob. While you may not use this as often as you do a saucepan, it's remarkably

21

versatile and worth the investment, particularly if you make a lot of pasta.

SKILLET: Choose a nonstick one to make cleanup easier, and make sure it is 8 to 10 inches in diameter. A skillet's straight sides make it ideal for preparing fried or scrambled eggs, frying burgers, and in a pinch, making pancakes.

BAKING EQUIPMENT: Even if you don't prepare dessert very often, it's worth investing in some baking tools and pans so you can make such treats as Three-Layer Carrot Cake, Red Velvet Cupcakes, and Rum Pecan Brownies. A glass 9-inch pie pan, a heavy-duty aluminum baking sheet or two, a 12-cup muffin tin, two or three 9-inch-round, 2-inch-deep aluminum cake pans, and a ceramic baking dish (perfect for Peach Cobbler) should be enough to get you started, and you can always add to your repertoire later by investing in fluted tart pans and loaf pans for baking quick breads and yeast loaves. A set of mixing bowls, a handheld electric mixer, an electric blender, and a food processor also are very useful to have.

ESSENTIAL KITCHEN TOOLS

Keep kitchen clutter at a minimum by having on hand just what you need. Here's a quick rundown of what you'll want to keep close when you cook.

A SET OF MEASURING CUPS: You'll actually do best if you get two sets, one for measuring liquids like water and oil, and one for measuring dry ingredients such as flour, bread crumbs, and grated cheese. Try to find a set of graduated cups so they can nest, thus taking up less space, or if you can get

ones with long handles, you'll be able to hang them on the wall where you can see them and grab them when you need them.

GARLIC PRESS: It's not essential, but if you often are pressed for time when you cook, this can be a real time-saver. Buy the best one that you can afford so you won't have to keep replacing an inferior model. Keep in mind that garlic put through a press will be stronger than garlic that is minced or chopped with a knife.

BISCUIT CUTTERS: Sure, you can use a drinking glass to cut out biscuits but these cutters are handy to have. Avoid the plastic ones, which don't cut as nicely, and pick up metal ones with a nice sharp edge.

SPATULA: You'll use this handy gadget for stirring puddings, scraping sauces out of saucepans, and whipping up batters for brownies, cakes, and muffins. Try to get a heatproof spatula with a nice long handle so it will reach into the bottom of the deepest mixing bowl or largest stockpot. Having a couple of these on hand makes perfect sense.

CANDY/FAT THERMOMETER: If you intend to fry vegetables or chicken, this is definitely an essential because you need to have your oil at the proper temperature before putting in the food or else risk sogginess. It will have a clip so that it can be attached right to the pan and a stay-cool plastic handle.

WHISKS: They're not expensive and they perform so many kitchen tasks—from beating cream and eggs to mixing thin batters—that it pays to pick up a couple of these. Hold them in your hands to see which ones have a comfortable grip, and look for those made of stainless steel.

KNIFE SMARTS

You don't need a fancy selection of knives in order to cook well. What you do need is an 8-inch chef's knife (for most kitchen tasks), a small paring knife (ideal for peeling and coring fruits and vegetables), and a serrated knife (to cut bread, slice tomatoes, and so forth). Get your knives sharpened at least once a year—if you don't have a good sharpener yourself, you can take them to the local hardware store and have them do it for you.

23

VEGETABLE STOCK

A good homemade stock is a basic necessity. It's like gas in a car: You can't get to your destination without it. Stock should have a clean, bright taste, and it should be very clear. You won't have any gelatinous quality to this stock since it's made only with vegetables, and without any meat. This is a pretty straightforward recipe but there are a few pointers to keep in mind. Be sure not to rush stock since it takes time for the flavors to develop. Your tomatoes should be fresh, not canned. Parsley is optional and so is the fennel. If you want to use it but can't find a fennel bulb, you may substitute 2 tablespoons of juniper berries or a pinch of allspice instead.

MAKES 2 QUARTS | LEVEL: LAYUP

2 medium ripe tomatoes, cored and chopped

$^{1}/_{2}$ medium yellow onion, chopped

1 leek, cleaned, trimmed, and chopped

2 shallots, chopped

4 garlic cloves, minced

2 celery stalks, chopped

1 carrot, chopped

1 parsnip chopped (optional)

1 medium fennel bulb, chopped (optional)

1 small bunch curly parsley, stemmed (optional)

1 teaspoon dried thyme (or 3 sprigs fresh thyme)

2 bay leaves

1 tablespoon freshly ground black pepper

Salt to taste

1. In a 4- or 5-quart Dutch oven, combine the tomatoes, onion, leek, shallots, garlic, celery, carrot, parsnip, and fennel (if using). Pour in 8 cups of cold water. Turn the heat to medium-low, and bring the liquid to a boil. As soon as it boils, reduce the heat to a simmer. As froth rises to the surface, skim it off with a skimmer, if you have one, or just with a large slotted spoon. Add the parsley (if using), thyme, bay leaves, pepper, and salt.

24

2. Simmer the stock, uncovered, for about 2 hours, continuing to occasionally skim off and discarding the froth from the surface. Pour the stock through a strainer, pressing down on the vegetables, into a large container. You can discard the vegetables or use them in a cream of vegetable soup. Allow the stock to cool, uncovered, for about an hour, than transfer it to a couple of smaller containers. Refrigerate it for up to a week, or freeze it for up to a month.

> " My first real experience with Chef Max in the kitchen was when we made this stock together. I just remember him saying that you can't achieve a great dish or sauce without a great stock. This is the best stock I've ever had."

CHICKEN STOCK

A great basic stock, this can be divided into smaller containers and frozen for up to three months. Use the chicken in a salad such as the Salad Trio (page 97), or make a great chicken sandwich. This stock makes the best soup ever.

MAKES ABOUT 6 CUPS | LEVEL: LAYUP

3 tablespoons extra-virgin olive oil

2 large yellow onions, diced

2 celery stalks, diced

2 carrots, chopped

1 leek, cleaned, trimmed, and sliced into thin strips

4 garlic cloves, minced

3 sprigs fresh thyme

3 bay leaves

3 sprigs fresh dill

3 sprigs fresh parsley

Kosher salt and freshly ground black pepper to taste

4-pound chicken, whole

1. In a large 4- to 6-quart stockpot, heat the olive oil on medium heat for 1 minute. Add the onion, celery, carrot, leek, garlic, thyme, bay leaves, dill, and parsley. Season the vegetables with salt and pepper. Sauté the vegetables for about 15 minutes, or until they are soft.

2. Carefully add the chicken to the stockpot. Pour in 8 cups of water. Bring the liquid to a boil over medium heat, reduce the heat to low, and simmer the stock for about $1^1/_2$ hours, occasionally skimming the foam from the surface, or until the chicken is thoroughly cooked.

3. Cool the chicken in the stock for about an hour. Remove the chicken from the pot and, when cool enough to handle, remove the meat from the bones. Discard the skin and the bones, and use the chicken in sandwiches, salad, or soup. Strain the stock, discarding the vegetables. Pour the stock into containers and refrigerate for up to a week. You can also freeze this stock for up to 3 months.

27

MARINARA SAUCE

The flavors are not overbearing in this clean, healthy, and versatile sauce. It's a "mother" sauce that you can do a lot with. Turn it into a tomato bisque, or use it as a base for a chicken stew. Or change up the flavor by adding olives, capers, and artichokes, or maybe vodka and cream. Make this sauce a day ahead of time, cool slightly, then cover and refrigerate. To rewarm, heat the sauce over medium heat, stirring gently.

SERVES 4 (ABOUT 1½ QUARTS) | LEVEL: LAYUP

¼ cup extra-virgin olive oil

1 small yellow onion, roughly chopped

1 garlic clove, roughly chopped

1 celery stalk, roughly chopped

1 carrot, roughly chopped

1 teaspoon sea salt, or to taste

½ teaspoon freshly ground black pepper, or to taste

2 32-ounce cans crushed tomatoes

4 fresh basil leaves

1 bay leaf

1. In a large pot, heat the oil for 30 seconds on medium-high. Add the onion and garlic and cook, stirring often, until the onion is translucent. This should take about 5 minutes. Add the celery, carrot, and ½ teaspoon each of salt and pepper.

2. Once all the vegetables are soft, which should take about 10 minutes, add the crushed tomatoes, basil, and bay leaf. Simmer, uncovered, over low heat for about 1 hour or until the sauce thickens.

3. Remove and discard the bay leaf. Taste the sauce, and add the remaining salt and additional pepper as needed.

28

" This is an Italian grandmother's favorite sauce, and in our kitchen, it's the one sauce that my kids love with their pasta. I'm not a real tomato fan, but I do like chicken parm, which calls for marinara."

CREAM SAUCE

Another classic, rich sauce that is a good one to have in your repertoire. Leftover roux can be used to thicken chicken noodle soup or vegetable soup, or to enrich and thicken any number of sauces. The roux will keep, tightly covered, for 2 or 3 weeks in the refrigerator.

MAKES ABOUT 3 CUPS | LEVEL: JUMP SHOT

For the roux:

1½ cups butter

2 cups all-purpose flour

For the sauce:

2 tablespoons extra-virgin olive oil

1 shallot, minced

2 garlic cloves, minced

1 bay leaf

1 cup dry white wine

2 cups heavy cream

Kosher salt and freshly ground black pepper to taste

1. Make the roux: In a heavy medium saucepan, melt the butter over low heat. Slowly add the flour. Cook, stirring or whisking constantly over low heat, until the roux is thick and smooth. Set the roux aside.

2. Make the sauce: Preheat a medium saucepan over medium-high heat for 1 minute. Add the olive oil, shallot, garlic, and bay leaf, and cook for 2 minutes, stirring.

3. Stir in the wine, heavy cream, and salt and pepper, and continue to cook, stirring constantly, for 2 minutes. Remove the bay leaf. Whisk in 1 tablespoon of the roux and continue to cook the sauce, stirring constantly, until it is slightly thickened. When the sauce coats the back of a spoon, it's perfectly done.

30

HERB BUTTER

The fresh herbs really bring out the best in this butter, so don't substitute dried ones if you can get fresh. Herb butter is delicious with steaks, fish, chicken, and savory pastries like biscuits or croissants. Whatever you opt to spread or melt it on, be sure to refrigerate it for at least 30 minutes before you serve. This not only firms the butter, but it allows the delicious herb flavor to permeate it. Using salted butter means that you won't need to add salt.

MAKES 1 LARGE LOG, SERVING AT LEAST 12 | LEVEL: LAYUP

2 pounds (8 sticks) salted butter, softened

1 tablespoon stemmed, chopped fresh cilantro

1 tablespoon finely chopped shallot

1 tablespoon finely chopped garlic

1 tablespoon chopped fresh rosemary

1 tablespoon chopped fresh thyme

1 tablespoon honey

1. In a large bowl, combine the softened butter, cilantro, shallot, garlic, rosemary, thyme, and honey. Using a large spoon, mix very well so that the herbs, garlic, and honey are evenly distributed throughout the butter.

2. Transfer the butter to a large sheet of plastic wrap. Using your hands or a spatula, form the butter into one large log or two small logs. Roll up the log tightly in the plastic wrap and refrigerate.

31

BARBECUE SAUCE

Barbecue sauce is so much better when you make it yourself! This is delicious on beef or just about any type of poultry. Store it in the refrigerator, tightly covered, and use it within a week.

MAKES 1¾ CUPS | LEVEL: LAYUP

1 cup ketchup

3 teaspoons dry mustard

½ cup apple cider vinegar

¼ cup agave nectar

1 garlic clove, minced

½ teaspoon liquid smoke

Pinch of kosher salt

3 tablespoons molasses

Juice of 1 lime

1 teaspoon soy sauce

¼ cup hot sauce, or to taste

1. In a medium saucepan, whisk the ketchup, dry mustard, apple cider vinegar, agave nectar, garlic, liquid smoke, salt, molasses, lime juice, soy sauce, and hot sauce.

2. Bring to a simmer over medium heat, reduce the heat to low, and cook for 5 minutes or until thick and smooth. Allow the sauce to cool, then transfer it to a container and refrigerate, tightly covered.

32

CAESAR DRESSING

In this dressing, which is pretty easy to whip up once you get all the ingredients together, the raw egg yolk is replaced with a bit of mayonnaise. The trick to Caesar dressing is to add the olive oil very slowly so that the dressing stays nice and creamy. If it "breaks," just add a little bit more mayonnaise and blend well. Your dressing will still be delicious!

SERVES 6 TO 8 | LEVEL: JUMP SHOT

6 garlic cloves, peeled

1 tablespoon Dijon mustard

1 tablespoon Champagne vinegar

1 teaspoon salt

2 tablespoons mayonnaise

$^1/_2$ cup extra-virgin olive oil

$^1/_4$ cup freshly grated Parmesan cheese

$^1/_4$ teaspoon freshly ground black pepper, or to taste

Freshly squeezed lemon juice, to taste

1 minced anchovy fillet (optional)

1. In an electric blender, combine the garlic cloves, Dijon mustard, champagne vinegar, and $^1/_2$ teaspoon salt. Blend until thoroughly mixed.

2. Add the mayonnaise and blend again, until the mixture is thick. Add the olive oil slowly, blend well, and add the Parmesan cheese. Blend until smooth.

3. Using a spatula, scrape the dressing into a small bowl and season it to taste with the remaining salt, pepper, and lemon juice. If you'd like your dressing to have a deeper, saltier taste, stir in the minced anchovy fillet. Store the dressing in the refrigerator, tightly covered, and use within several days.

33

"This is where I do my thing and let Chef have a break. He helped me master this dressing so I could make my favorite salad."

SIMPLE VINAIGRETTE

This basic vinaigrette is good on all kinds of green salads, and you could even use it as a marinade for chicken or fish. Prepared ahead of time, this vinaigrette will keep for up to week in a tightly covered container in the refrigerator.

MAKES 1¼ CUPS | LEVEL: LAYUP

1 cup extra-virgin olive oil

¼ cup Champagne vinegar

2 garlic cloves, peeled

1 shallot, peeled and trimmed

1 tablespoon honey

2 teaspoons fresh cilantro leaves, stemmed

1 teaspoon chopped fresh tarragon

Kosher salt and freshly ground black pepper to taste

1. In an electric blender, combine the olive oil, vinegar, garlic, shallot, honey, cilantro, and tarragon. Season with a little salt and pepper.

2. Blend the vinaigrette until it is well mixed and thoroughly emulsified. Transfer it to a container with a tightly fitting lid, cover, and refrigerate.

TROPICAL FRUIT RELISH

Serve this colorful, healthy relish with your favorite protein or as a snack. It's especially good with fish. You'll note that the instructions call for the mint to be cut into chiffonade. In French, this word means "made of rags," but in cooking, it means when vegetables are cut into very thin strips or shreds (see Some Useful Cooking Terms, page 15).

SERVES 4 TO 6 | LEVEL: LAYUP

$1/2$ large pineapple, cored and diced

1 large peach, peeled, pitted, and diced

1 small papaya, peeled, pitted, and diced

1 kiwi, peeled and diced

1 large mango, peeled, pitted, and diced

4 strawberries, hulled and sliced

$1/4$ cup extra-virgin olive oil

3 mint leaves, cut into chiffonade

$1/4$ bunch chopped fresh cilantro, leaves only, stemmed

2 tablespoons agave nectar

2 tablespoons Champagne vinegar

1. In a large mixing bowl, combine the pineapple, peach, papaya, kiwi, mango, and strawberries.

2. To make the dressing, in a small bowl, whisk the olive oil, mint, cilantro, agave nectar, and Champagne vinegar. Pour the dressing over the fruit and chill the relish for 30 minutes before serving.

FRESH TOMATO SALSA

Another great dish to keep in the fridge, this salsa is amazing on fish, chicken, salads, or just with some nice chips. Best stored in a Mason jar, it will last for at least a week if you keep it covered and chilled. This versatile recipe lends itself to different variations. You'll be surprised how many different ways you can make it. Go Caribbean by adding some avocado. For a Mexican flavor, add some black beans, or stir in some chopped pineapple for a truly tropical flavor. And if you don't have agave, use honey or sugar instead.

SERVES 4 TO 6 | LEVEL: LAYUP

2 large beefsteak tomatoes, cored and diced

2 garlic cloves, minced

3 tablespoons stemmed, chopped fresh cilantro

3 tablespoons extra-virgin olive oil

¼ red medium onion, diced

Juice of 1 lime

1 tablespoon agave nectar

1 teaspoon ground cumin

Kosher salt and freshly ground black pepper to taste

1. In a medium mixing bowl, combine the diced tomato, garlic, cilantro, olive oil, red onion, lime juice, agave nectar, cumin, salt, and pepper.

2. Stir the salsa until all ingredients are well combined. Taste, and add extra salt and pepper if needed.

3. Store the salsa in a covered container in the refrigerator.

For this bright, sassy salsa to taste its best, choose the ripest beefsteak tomatoes you can find. These large, bright-red tomatoes, which are vaguely elliptical in shape, are juicy, flavorful, and easy to find. If, after buying the tomatoes, you find yourself short of time and needing to hold off on making the salsa, resist the urge to refrigerate the tomatoes. They really retain their best flavor when stored at room temperature, and will keep for a few days out of the fridge.

36

" What an amazing simple dish,
except for when I almost cut
my fingers off making it the
first time! My advice: Make sure
you've mastered your knife skills,
and take it slow. Once you know
how to do it, this is a truly fun
salsa to make."

37

ROASTED CORN RELISH

The best time to enjoy this is in the summer, when corn is fresh and sweet. Be sure to make it a couple of hours ahead so the flavors can mingle. Toss this relish with greens for a terrific salad, or serve it alongside grilled chicken or fish.

SERVES 4 TO 6 | LEVEL: JUMP SHOT

3 ears corn, husked, all silk removed

$^1/_4$ cup extra-virgin olive oil

3 tablespoon chopped red onion

1 tablespoon stemmed, chopped fresh cilantro

$^1/_4$ diced bell pepper

1 tablespoon minced jalapeño chile

2 garlic cloves, minced

Juice of $^1/_2$ lemon

Kosher salt and freshly ground black pepper to taste

1. Preheat a grill or a grill pan over medium-high heat for 1 or 2 minutes. Brush the corn with the olive oil.

39

2. Grill the corn on all sides, turning occasionally, for 3 to 5 minutes, or until grill marks appear. Set the corn aside for 30 minutes or until it comes to room temperature.

3. Cut the kernels from the ears of corn. Transfer the corn kernels to a medium bowl. Stir in the chopped onion, cilantro, bell pepper, chile, garlic, lemon juice, salt, and pepper.

4. When all the ingredients have been well incorporated, cover and chill the relish. Bring the relish to room temperature before serving.

40

CHEF MAX'S SPICE BLEND

When you want to add flavor fast, this spice blend is the answer. Make it in advance and store it in a Mason jar. It will keep at room temperature for weeks.

MAKES ¼ CUP | LEVEL: LAYUP

2 teaspoons garlic powder

2 teaspoons onion powder

2 teaspoons mild paprika

2 teaspoons ground cumin

2 teaspoons dried parsley

2 teaspoons brown sugar

1 teaspoon kosher salt

1 teaspoon freshly ground black pepper

1. In a medium mixing bowl, combine the garlic powder, onion powder, paprika, cumin, parsley, brown sugar, salt, and pepper. Stir until well mixed.

2. Transfer the spice blend to a Mason jar or another container with a tightly fitting lid. Cover and store in a cool, dry place.

41

WARM-UP

"AMAR'E

Growing up in a hectic household, breakfast was pretty much whatever I could find quickly. I was so busy between school and basketball that I didn't have much time to eat breakfast. I often just grabbed something on my way out the door.

Once I began playing pro basketball, I came to realize that I needed to eat a morning meal that would give me energy for the hours of practice I put in daily. But it wasn't until Chef Max came into my life that I really took breakfast seriously. I began to see that besides being a great way to start your morning, breakfast sets the tone for the entire day. If you have a morning meal with a proper balance of nutrition, you can keep your energy up for the rest of the day.

Since I do some sort of workout every morning both during the season and off-season, I have to make sure that I eat right so I am ready to push myself mentally and physically.

For me, variety at breakfast is important and I really like it when Chef Max switches things up so I don't eat the same thing day in and day out. One of my favorite ways to start the day is with freshly made juice. Another great start for

me is a big bowl of oatmeal and a protein smoothie. I like to mix things up and use various fruits and greens in my smoothies.

As for our children, mornings are very busy. Chef Max prepares breakfast foods that are meant to sustain them as they go about their day. We encourage our children to eat a healthy breakfast of foods they love rather than sugary cereals.

During the week, we keep healthy breakfast options on hand for the kids, like a yogurt and granola parfait or a bowl of oatmeal with berries. On the weekends, I love to make a big breakfast for the family. I make the best Spanish omelets, and I serve these with turkey bacon and whole-wheat toast.

Of course, breakfast time is also when Alexis and I help the kids review for spelling tests and make sure they are ready for whatever their school day may bring. Breakfast is very busy in our household, but I love it. I believe that one of the most important things for me and Alexis is to instill healthy eating habits in our children. Breakfast is a great place to start.

MAX "

Breakfast really *is* the most important meal of the day. And when Amar'e is in season, he takes this meal very seriously. He might have two green juices to start the day, and a vegetable omelet or a burrito, around 7:00 a.m. Though he doesn't need coffee to get his morning started, he will have a cup of green tea. A fruit plate that I make up for him in the morning is stashed in the refrigerator so he can snack on this when he wants to.

On a game day, after breakfast Amar'e goes back to bed and sleeps until around noon. He gets up and has a light lunch and maybe has a massage. Then it's back to bed for a quick nap because he needs to be up at around 3:00 p.m. for his pregame meal. Amar'e won't eat after that until around 11:00 p.m., when he has his postgame dinner.

To avoid breakfast boredom, it's important to vary what you serve in the morn-

45

ing. When I first started to cook breakfast for Amar'e and his family, they were pretty much eating the same thing every day. For the kids, this meant pancakes or waffles they could pop in the toaster, but nothing outside the box. Amar'e would have eggs and maybe turkey bacon, but there weren't exactly any vegetables peeking out of those omelets and frittatas.

My goal was to heighten their palates while still keeping things tasty and healthy. Instead of plain eggs, I'd put avocado in an omelet. Or I'd make a frittata with all different kinds of vegetables, like broccolini and mushrooms. On the weekends, I started showing Amar'e how to scramble an egg, make a frittata, roll a burrito.

Although the weekday mornings are so hectic that he doesn't have time to show off his culinary skills, he now makes breakfast for his family on weekends.

Omelets are just one of the dishes he has mastered, and one of his favorites (turkey bacon and spinach) is now a favorite with the kids.

They also like it when their dad makes them scrambled eggs loaded with cheese and turkey bacon, homemade waffles, raisin bran French toast, and breakfast burritos. Even though they eat simply in the morning during the week, I think it's safe to say that on the weekends, Amar'e's kids take breakfast just about as seriously as he does.

46

GYM SHORTS

With four kids in the house, our mornings
are hectic since everyone has to get
dressed, have breakfast, and get ready
for school, which starts quite early.
Somehow, though, everything runs
smoothly, thanks to my wife, Alexis. She
is incredibly organized and makes it all
look very simple, even though it's not!

While Alexis focuses on organizing everyone and making sure they are
dressed, I make sure they get a healthy and strong start to the day with a
well-balanced breakfast that we eat together as a family. We believe in keeping
our mornings as low-key and low-maintenance as possible so that the kids start
the day feeling calm, focused, and ready to do their very best.

Here are some shortcuts we follow to avoid morning may-
hem.

• Nothing short-circuits a morning more quickly than a cranky, overtired
child. Set and enforce a regular bedtime and make it an early one since
kids need a surprising lot of sleep. To help them get in the mood for sleep,
establish a bedtime routine and stick to it. Follow the same schedule each
night.

• Make sure all the children's clothes are laid out the night before. The
clothes should be agreed upon in advance. Get the backpacks packed and
the shoes lined up and ready to go, too. Nothing can derail a morning
schedule faster than a futile hunt for a missing sneaker that must be
worn in phys ed class that day.

•Organize yourself, too, by making sure your house and car keys are kept in the same place at all times.

•Install a large calendar, keep it up to date, and fill in all important events from the school calendar onto this master calendar. Look at the calendar at night to make sure anything that will be needed the next day (permission slips, gym clothes, library books) is ready to go.

•Consider staggering the morning wake-up calls. If you've got one kid who dawdles and daydreams her way through the morning and a go-getter who can power through the a.m. routine in mere minutes, wake your dawdler, give him your time and attention, and then wake up his sibling. You'll feel a lot less frazzled if you have to deal with only one or two temperaments at a time.

•Once they are school-age, transfer to your children some of the responsibility of getting up in the morning. You might even give them an alarm clock and suggest that they start setting it and waking themselves.

•Keep breakfast choices simple on weekday mornings. Offer just a couple of options and make sure none of them take more than three minutes to prepare.

CALIFORNIA FRITTATA

Made with freshly picked zucchini, bell peppers, and herbs, this frittata tastes like the essence of California. Be sure to cut the vegetables into fairly small, uniformly sized pieces so they will cook evenly—and look pretty.

SERVES 6 TO 8 | LEVEL: JUMP SHOT

1 small zucchini, cut into 1-inch dice

1 red bell pepper, cored, seeded, and cut into 1½-inch dice

1 yellow bell pepper, cored, seeded, and cut into 1½-inch dice

1 large red onion, cut into 1½-inch dice

⅓ cup extra-virgin olive oil

2½ teaspoons kosher salt

1 teaspoon freshly ground black pepper

2 large cloves garlic, minced

12 eggs

¼ cup half-and-half

¼ cup freshly grated Parmesan cheese

1 tablespoon unsalted butter

⅓ cup chopped scallion, white and green parts (3 scallions)

¼ cup grated Gruyère cheese

1. Preheat the oven to 425°F.

2. Combine the zucchini, bell peppers, and red onion on a sheet pan. Drizzle with the olive oil, sprinkle with 1½ teaspoons salt and ½ teaspoon pepper, and toss well. Bake for about 15 minutes or until softened and browned.

3. Add the garlic, toss again, and bake for another 15 minutes. Remove from the oven and reduce the oven heat to 350°F.

4. In a large bowl, whisk the eggs, half-and-half, Parmesan cheese, 1 teaspoon salt, and ½ teaspoon pepper.

5. In a deep, 10-inch ovenproof sauté pan over medium-low heat, melt the butter. Add the scallions and sauté them for 1 minute. Add the roasted vegetables to the pan and toss with the scallions.

49

6. Pour the egg mixture over the vegetables and cook for 2 minutes over medium-low heat without stirring. Transfer the pan to the oven and bake the frittata for 15 to 20 minutes, until puffed and set in the middle. Sprinkle with the Gruyère and bake for another 3 minutes or until the cheese is just melted. Cut into 6 or 8 wedges and serve hot.

" When Chef Max and I were in California for about a week together, I remember days when I would be looking out of my bedroom window watching him pick herbs and vegetables from the garden and wondering what he was going to muster up that day. I love this frittata (or what I called it back then—an unfolded omelet)."

50

BREAKFAST BURRITOS

This energizing burrito is made with turkey sausage but you could certainly make it with pork sausage instead. For extra heat, add a few more chiles and additional chopped cilantro.

MAKES 4 | LEVEL: LAYUP

3 tablespoons extra-virgin olive oil

1 cup chopped yellow onion

8 ounces turkey breakfast sausage, crumbled

1 4-ounce can diced green chiles, drained

1 15.5-ounce can black beans, drained and rinsed

$^1/_2$ bunch cilantro, stemmed and chopped

6 large eggs, lightly beaten

Kosher salt and freshly ground black pepper to taste

6 12-inch flour tortillas

1 cup grated Mexican-blend Jack cheese

Sour cream and fresh salsa, for garnish

1. Heat a large nonstick skillet over medium heat for 1 minute. Add the olive oil and heat it for 1 minute. Add the onion to the pan and sauté it for 2 minutes. Add the sausage and sauté it until it loses its pink color. Drain off any excess liquid that has accumulated.

2. Add the green chiles, black beans, and cilantro. Stir until very warm. Add the eggs and stir them until they are firm. Sprinkle with some salt and pepper.

3. Heat the tortillas in the microwave for a few seconds, just until they are pliable. Arrange the tortillas on a clean work surface. Divide the egg mixture among the tortillas. Top the egg with some cheese. Roll up the burritos to enclose the filling, then cut each in half and serve them with sour cream and salsa.

53

"These burritos are actually one of my favorite dishes to make, though there is a funny story behind it. When I was the executive chef at a country club in Weston, Florida, the general manager wanted a breakfast burrito on his desk at 8 o'clock each morning. If it wasn't there, I would get a call and he would threaten to fire me. One day, I had had enough. I made 14 burritos and left them on his desk. It was my way of giving him two weeks' notice! It wasn't long after that that I began thinking of moving out of Florida and becoming a personal chef."

" Now we are talking about having a little bit of everything from the fridge, diced and rolled up in a tortilla. This is an easy recipe for me and you can definitely master it, too."

MIXED BERRY PARFAIT

This is a favorite with the kids, and would make a nice, quick breakfast for when you're in a hurry. If you don't like fresh mint, simply leave it off.

2 cups strawberries, sliced

2 cups blueberries

1 nectarine, peeled, pitted, and chopped

1 teaspoon agave nectar

Juice of half an orange

3 fresh mint leaves, chopped

Pinch of cinnamon

1 teaspoon vanilla extract

$1/2$ cup granola

2 cups plain or vanilla yogurt (nonfat or low-fat)

4 fresh mint leaves, for garnish

1. In a large bowl, combine the strawberries, blueberries, and nectarine.

2. Stir in the agave nectar, orange juice, mint, cinnamon, and vanilla. Toss gently.

3. In 4 parfait dishes, layer about one eighth of the fruit mixture, then 1 tablespoon of granola, and then one quarter cup of yogurt. Repeat the layers once. Garnish each parfait with a fresh mint leaf. Serve immediately.

55

TROPICAL SMOOTHIES

There's nothing like a fresh fruit smoothie to get your day started, especially when it tastes like the refreshing flavors of the Caribbean. This makes enough for everyone in the family to have a glassful, and it's so sweet and delicious that it could be a milkshake.

SERVES 6 | LEVEL: LAYUP

2 to 3 cups ice cubes

1 large ripe mango, peeled and diced

3 ripe bananas, peeled and chopped

12 strawberries, hulled and quartered

1/4 cup raspberries

3 kiwis, peeled and chopped

1/2 cup honey

1 cup vanilla yogurt (nonfat or low-fat)

1 cup mango nectar

1 cup low-fat whipped cream for topping the smoothies

Fresh mint sprigs for garnish

1. Place the ice cubes a large blender. Top with the mango, banana, strawberries, raspberries, and kiwi. Blend briefly, for about 30 seconds.

2. Add the honey, yogurt, and mango nectar. Blend at high speed until all the ingredients are well incorporated.

3. Pour into tall glasses. Top each serving with low-fat whipped cream and mint sprigs. Refrigerate until ready to serve.

STAT JUICE

You will need one of those big juicers in order to make this vitamin-packed drink, and if you plan on investing in one, it pays to get a good one. The Vita Juicer is an excellent juicer. By the way, STAT is the acronym for Stand Tall and Talented (the name for Amare's children's book series).

SERVES 6 TO 8 | LEVEL: LAYUP

1 pound kale, washed and trimmed

$1/2$ ripe pineapple, peeled, cored, and diced

1 celery stalk, trimmed and cut into large pieces

2 cucumbers, peeled and cut into large pieces

2 apples, peeled, cored, and quartered

$1/4$-inch piece ginger, peeled

1 lemon, peeled and quartered

1. Using a large juicer, extract the juice from the kale, pineapple, celery, cucumber, apple, ginger, and lemon.

2. Pour the juice into a large cocktail shaker and shake with some ice cubes.

3. Serve the juice in tall glasses, over ice if desired.

STEAK AND EGGS

This energizing, protein-packed breakfast will soon become a favorite at your house. Classic hollandaise sauce is made with butter, egg yolks, and lemon, but this gets a twist by adding lime juice, cilantro, and a little Tabasco sauce.

SERVES 6 | LEVEL: SLAM DUNK

For the hollandaise sauce:

4 large egg yolks

1 cup (2 sticks) butter, melted and hot

1 teaspoon lime juice

1 teaspoon stemmed, chopped fresh cilantro

2 dashes Tabasco sauce

For the steaks:

6 6-ounce rib eye steaks

2 cups all-purpose flour

2 teaspoons onion powder

2 teaspoons garlic powder

2 teaspoons Chef Max's Spice Blend (page 41)

1 or 2 eggs, lightly beaten

1 cup freshly grated Parmesan cheese

1 tablespoon chopped fresh curly parsley

3 cups panko bread crumbs

1/2 cup extra-virgin olive oil

For the eggs:

2 tablespoons extra-virgin olive oil

6 large eggs

Kosher salt and freshly ground black pepper to taste

1. Make the hollandaise sauce: Place the egg yolks in a blender and blend on low for 5 seconds. Add the butter slowly and blend well. Add the lime juice, cilantro, and Tabasco, and blend again. Set aside the hollandaise sauce while you make the steak and eggs.

2. Make the steaks: Using a meat mallet or a heavy plate, pound the steaks very thin. In a large, shallow plate, combine the flour, onion powder, garlic powder, and Chef Max's Spice Blend. In a shallow bowl, whisk the egg with the Parmesan cheese and the chopped parsley. Place the panko bread crumbs

60

on a third shallow plate. Dip the steaks into the flour mixture, then into the beaten egg mixture, and then into the panko bread crumbs. Make sure the steaks are well-coated with the panko bread crumbs.

3. Heat the olive oil in a 12-inch sauté pan over medium heat. Sauté the steaks for about 2 minutes per side or until they are medium-rare (or to desired degree of doneness). Remove the steaks from the pan.

4. Make the eggs: Preheat a second sauté pan over medium heat for 1 minute. Add the olive oil and swirl it around so that it coats the bottom of the pan. Crack the eggs into the pan. Fry them on 1 side for about 3 minutes, until the whites are cooked and the yolks are still bright and runny. Sprinkle the eggs with some salt and pepper.

5. Arrange the steaks on serving plates, and top each with a fried egg. Stir the hollandaise sauce with a spoon and if it is too thick, add a few teaspoons of water. It should be thin enough to pour. Drizzle some of the hollandaise sauce over each serving of steak and eggs.

CHEESE GRITS

There's nothing like piping hot grits to start off the day on the right foot. While they're traditional in the South, grits is one breakfast that Northerners are happy to adopt. Some people season their grits with no more than a pat of butter, but this dish gets some extra kick with scallion, white pepper, and some cheese.

SERVES 6 | LEVEL: LAYUP

Kosher salt to taste

$1^1/_2$ cups quick-cooking grits

1 cup heavy cream

1 cup shredded cheddar cheese

3 tablespoons chopped scallion (white and light green parts)

2 teaspoons unsalted butter

Pinch of white pepper

1. Bring 3 cups of water and a pinch of salt to a boil in a large saucepan.

2. Slowly whisk in the grits, reduce the heat to medium, and cook for 5 to 6 minutes or until tender.

3. Whisk in the heavy cream and cook for another 2 minutes. Remove the saucepan from the heat. Add in the cheddar cheese, scallion, butter, and pepper. Stir until the cheese and butter are melted. Serve hot.

63

HOMEMADE WHEAT BUTTERMILK BISCUITS

These are delicious not just for breakfast but for afternoon tea, with some good preserves. Or you could serve them with a frittata (or even make a sandwich with some of the frittata as your filling).

MAKES 8 | LEVEL: JUMP SHOT

1 cup whole-wheat flour

1 cup all-purpose flour

1 teaspoon baking powder

1/2 teaspoon baking soda

2 teaspoons sugar

1/2 teaspoon kosher salt

1/2 cup (1 stick) unsalted butter, chilled and cut into pieces

1 cup well-chilled buttermilk

1. Preheat the oven to 450°F.

2. In a large bowl, whisk the whole-wheat flour, all-purpose flour, baking powder, baking soda, sugar, and salt. Add the butter. Rub the mixture with your fingers until it resembles coarse meal. Stir the buttermilk into the dry ingredients until the flour mixture is moistened.

3. Turn the dough out onto a lightly floured surface and knead it lightly with the heel of your hand 4 or 5 times. Roll or pat the dough out to about a 1-inch thickness.

4. Cut the dough into biscuits, using a 3-inch biscuit cutter or a drinking glass. Reroll the dough scraps to make more biscuits. Arrange them evenly on an ungreased baking sheet. Bake the biscuits for 12 to 14 minutes, or until brown.

64

"This was a tough one for me at first. Measuring wasn't my thing. I thought you could just add a little of this and a little of that but my biscuits came out like pancakes. Make sure you follow the directions!"

65

WARM-UP

CHEESE AND CHIVE BISCUITS WITH GARLIC AND HONEY TOPPING

These easy-to-make biscuits, which taste great on their own or with various egg dishes, are best made with fresh chives. If you don't have any, you can substitute scallions (just the green part). Serve these biscuits warm, with plenty of butter.

MAKES 12 | LEVEL: JUMP SHOT

For the biscuits:

Butter, oil, or cooking spray for the baking sheet

3 cups all-purpose flour, plus more for sprinkling on the work surface

1 tablespoon baking powder

2 teaspoons sugar

1 teaspoon baking soda

1 teaspoon kosher salt

$1/2$ cup (1 stick) unsalted butter, chilled, cut into pieces

1 cup buttermilk

1 cup grated cheddar cheese

$1/4$ cup chopped fresh chives

For the topping:

4 tablespoons unsalted butter

2 garlic cloves, chopped

2 tablespoons honey

1. Position an oven rack in the center of the oven and preheat the oven to 450°F.

2. Coat a large baking sheet with butter, oil, or cooking spray.

3. In a large bowl, whisk the flour, baking powder, sugar, baking soda, and salt. Add the butter. With your fingers or a pastry blender, cut it into the flour until the mixture resembles coarse meal.

4. Using a large spatula, fold the buttermilk into the flour mixture until all the flour is moistened. Add the cheese and chives, and mix well.

66

5. Sprinkle a few tablespoons of flour on a work surface. Turn the dough out onto the work surface and knead it lightly two or three times with the palms of your hands. When the dough comes together and is fairly smooth, pat it until it is about 1 inch thick.

6. Using a 3-inch-round biscuit cutter, cut out biscuits and place them onto the baking sheet. Reroll the scraps and make more biscuits.

7. Bake the biscuits for 10 to 15 minutes or until they are lightly golden brown and firm to the touch. Remove the biscuits from the oven.

8. Make the topping: In a small saucepan, melt the butter over low heat. Add the garlic and the honey. Stir very well. Using a pastry brush, coat the biscuits with the garlic-honey glaze.

67

SWEET POTATO WAFFLES

Waffles with a Southern accent—breakfast doesn't get any better. If there are any leftovers, wrap and refrigerate them because they're terrific toasted for breakfast the next morning. Since waffle irons vary so much in size, it's important to follow your waffle iron's specific instructions about how much batter to use for each waffle. Generally speaking, it takes around ¾ cup to make one waffle.

SERVES 4 TO 6 | LEVEL: JUMP SHOT

2 large eggs, lightly beaten

2 cups all-purpose flour

½ cup vegetable oil

1 tablespoon sugar

¼ teaspoon baking powder

¼ teaspoon kosher salt

1 teaspoon vanilla extract

1 teaspoon pumpkin pie spice

1 cup canned (15-ounce), mashed sweet potatoes

Nonstick cooking spray for the waffle iron

Maple syrup

1. Preheat a waffle iron.

2. In a large bowl, with a handheld electric mixer set on medium, beat together the eggs, flour, oil, sugar, baking powder, salt, vanilla, and pumpkin pie spice. When the batter is smooth, stir in the mashed sweet potato.

3. Spray the waffle iron with the nonstick cooking spray. Pour approximately ¾ to 1 cup of the batter into the center of the waffle iron and close the top. Follow the instructions for your waffle iron, baking the waffles until they are crisp and hot.

4. Remove the waffles from the waffle iron and repeat this process with the remaining batter. Serve hot, with maple syrup.

68

BREAK FOR LUNCH

....

CURRIED CHICKEN AND RICE SOUP 74

TOMATO BISQUE 77

ROASTED VEGETABLE AND GOAT CHEESE FLATBREADS 79

THE ULTIMATE BURGER 82

GRILLED VEGETABLE WRAPS 84

TUNA WRAPS WITH MANDARIN ORANGES
AND SWEET CHILI SAUCE 86

BRIE AND MOZZARELLA SANDWICHES 88

ROASTED TURKEY AND CUCUMBER SANDWICHES 90

MINI FISH TACOS WITH CILANTRO CRÈME FRAÎCHE 92

SALMON CAKES WITH GARLIC AIOLI 95

SALAD TRIO 97

CALIFORNIA COBB SALAD 99

....

"AMAR'E

When I was growing up, the best packed lunch ever meant a sandwich, a piece of fruit, milk, and some sort of treat like crackers or chips. It was basic, but it worked. My kids eat a lunch that is provided by their school, so we don't pack their lunches in the morning. But when they get home, they are ravenous. That's when they like to eat a snack they call Turtle Sandwiches (page 268): Marshmallow Fluff, Nutella, peanut butter, jelly, and banana slices on bread.

You won't find me eating this, though. I may have a steak with a big salad or what I call the Salad Trio (page 97), which consists of a scoop each of egg salad, tuna salad, and chicken salad. With a big fruit platter and a STAT Juice (page 59), it's all I need. Alexis and the kids like the Salad Trio, too. The kids scoop it up with crackers, and Alexis uses it to make a sandwich.

On Saturdays, which is Chef Max's day off, lunch is more leisurely. We like to observe the Sabbath by spending time together as a family. Part of the day is spent running the kids to practices and games, so I try to make a big lunch for them so they can fuel up. Sometimes on the weekends, we have friends over and when we do, we serve a pasta dish with a big salad. I think lunch foods should be the kinds of foods that you can enjoy in a relaxed setting with friends and family.

72

MAX "

For Amar'e, lunch wasn't always about making the time to eat good, balanced meals. With a long roster of volunteer commitments, social engagements, and team events, he often just did not have enough time for lunch to be a priority. He knew that he had to eat to keep up his energy level, but it wasn't unusual for him to just grab takeout or eat fast food.

Once I started to cook for him, I wanted to change his eating patterns and help him develop a healthy palate so that he would start to eat for energy at all times, including lunchtime. Now, on some days, he might have a small steak for lunch, along with a salad. Or salad might be the main course.

Lunchtime is a busy time for Amare's family on the weekends. On my day off, Amar'e really gets the chance to show off his culinary prowess by making the family a big lunch. In fact, it's probably when I'm not here that the family gets really creative about lunch. They like making all kinds of sandwiches with the cold cuts I stock in the refrigerator. But it's just as likely for Amar'e to make them all a big pot of soup. One of the kids' favorite lunches is homemade tomato bisque and grilled-cheese sandwiches. That is one of the meals he's mastered, and it's a go-to lunch for the whole family.

I think that lunch is a good time to change things up a little, to get inventive with the recipes. That's why this chapter is packed with many different kinds of recipes—one for every day of the week, and some left over.

73

CURRIED CHICKEN AND RICE SOUP

Curry powder and fresh thyme give this soup a delicious riff on chicken curry and rice, a lively flavor.

SERVES 6 | LEVEL: JUMP SHOT

1½ (3- to 4-pound) chickens, quartered

2 bay leaves

4 tablespoons curry powder

1 large yellow onion, diced

2 celery stalks, diced

2 carrots, diced

2 tablespoons tomato paste

5 sprigs fresh thyme, chopped

4 garlic cloves, chopped

1 cup cooked white beans, such as cannellini

¼ cup red bell pepper, cored, seeded, and chopped

¼ cup green bell pepper, cored, seeded, and chopped

¼ cup yellow bell pepper, cored, seeded, and chopped

¼ Scotch bonnet pepper, minced

1 cup uncooked jasmine rice

Kosher salt and freshly ground black pepper to taste

1. In a 3- or 4-quart saucepan or Dutch oven, bring 6 cups of water to a boil. Add the chicken pieces, bay leaves, and curry powder. Reduce the heat and simmer the chicken for about 1 hour or until it is fully cooked. Skim off any froth that accumulates as the chicken cooks.

2. Add the onion, celery, carrot, tomato paste, 3 sprigs of thyme, garlic, white beans, bell peppers, and Scotch bonnet pepper. Simmer the soup for another 15 minutes. Remove the bay leaves.

3. Add the rice to the saucepan and stir well. Cover the saucepan and simmer the soup for 20 minutes, or until the rice is tender. Season the soup with salt and pepper. Serve in large bowls, garnishing each serving with the remaining chopped thyme.

> "I love Caribbean and Jamaican food, and I love chicken curry with rice. So of course, this soup quickly became one of my favorites."

OUT OF BOUNDS

On a serene, pastoral 200-acre farm in New York's Hudson Valley, a four-bedroom log cabin looks out over lush apple and peach orchards. Fields are being planted with a variety of vegetable crops and chickens, ducks, sheep, and goats will soon be calling this place home. Welcome to the newly christened Stoudemire Farm, soon to be an online market for everything from homemade jams and jellies to fresh vegetables to cheeses and high-end meats. Once the new farm is up and running, maple syrup from its many maple trees will be marketed as well.

We are both committed to using locally grown produce and meat as often as possible, so purchasing a farm that could supply us with fruits, vegetables, poultry, and red meat was a natural move. Not only do we want to be more environmentally conscious in our cooking, we want to show others the way as well. We're very excited about our new venture! Under Max's supervision, the farm project is growing by leaps and bounds and should be ready for business by this summer.

76

TOMATO BISQUE

The tomatoes are "hidden" in this soup, which is a great way to get kids to eat more vegetables. With grilled-cheese sandwiches, Tomato Bisque makes a perfect lunch in the fall and winter months.

SERVES 4 TO 6 | LEVEL: JUMP SHOT

6 large, ripe tomatoes, cored and halved

1/2 cup extra-virgin olive oil

1 teaspoon chopped fresh thyme

Sea salt to taste

4 garlic cloves, minced

2 shallots, chopped

2 bay leaves

4 fresh basil leaves, cut into chiffonade

1/4 cup (1/2 stick) unsalted butter

1/4 cup all-purpose flour

1/2 cup sherry

1 cup heavy cream

1 cup Chicken Stock (page 27)

Freshly ground black pepper to taste

Freshly grated Parmesan cheese, for garnish

1. Preheat the oven to 400°F.

2. In a large bowl, toss the tomato halves with $1/4$ cup of the olive oil, $1/2$ teaspoon of the thyme, $1/2$ teaspoon sea salt, and half the garlic. Transfer the tomatoes to a large baking sheet, spread them out evenly, and roast them in the oven for 35 minutes or until softened. Set the tomatoes aside to cool.

3. Set a 4-quart saucepan or a Dutch oven over medium heat and preheat it for 2 minutes. Add the remaining $1/4$ cup olive oil, $1/2$ teaspoon thyme, garlic, and the chopped shallot, bay leaves, and half the basil. Sauté the mixture for 2 minutes. Add the butter and the flour and continue to cook, stirring, for 2 to 3 minutes. Remove the bay leaves. Whisk in the sherry, heavy cream, and chicken stock. Simmer, stirring constantly, for 3 minutes or until slightly thickened. Transfer the cream mixture to a large bowl.

4. In a large blender, puree half of the roasted tomatoes. Add half of the cream mixture to the blender, and puree until the tomatoes and the cream mixture are well-incorporated. Return this mixture to the stockpot. Puree the remaining roasted tomatoes and cream mixture. Return this mixture to the stockpot. Stir the soup thoroughly to blend it well.

5. Heat the soup over low heat until it is very hot. Taste, and add salt and pepper as needed. Serve the soup in bowls, soup cups, or hollowed out bread topped with Parmesan cheese and the remaining basil.

 This is comfort food for me.
When it's not a game day, I like
to sit on the couch and eat this soup
with a grilled-cheese sandwich."

ROASTED VEGETABLE AND GOAT CHEESE FLATBREADS

This recipe is loaded with vegetables for the kids—feel free to add any you have on hand. If you have a pizza board, arrange the flatbreads on this when it's time to serve. You can store leftover béchamel sauce, tightly covered, for up to 3 days.

SERVES 4 | LEVEL: JUMP SHOT

For the béchamel sauce:

4 tablespoons unsalted butter

$1/2$ medium yellow onion, chopped

3 tablespoons all-purpose flour

2 cups hot milk

1 teaspoon kosher salt

$1/4$ teaspoon nutmeg

For the flatbreads:

1 zucchini, diced

1 summer squash, diced

1 medium red onion, diced

1 red bell pepper, cored, seeded, and diced

1 yellow bell pepper, cored, seeded, and diced

1 portobello mushroom, diced

3 garlic cloves, chopped

$1/4$ cup extra-virgin olive oil

Kosher salt and freshly ground pepper to taste

4 flatbreads

2 cups freshly grated Parmesan cheese

3 ounces goat cheese, crumbled

$1/4$ pound feta cheese, crumbled

5 leaves fresh basil, cut into chiffonade

79

1. Make the béchamel sauce: In a medium saucepan, heat the butter over medium heat until melted. Add the onion and cook for 5 minutes, or until soft. Add the flour and cook, stirring, until it turns light brown. Whisk the hot milk into the flour mixture and cook, stirring, for 10 minutes or until thickened and smooth. Season the sauce with the salt and the nutmeg.

2. Preheat the oven to 450°F.

3. Make the flatbreads: In a large bowl, combine the zucchini, summer squash, onion, red and yellow bell pepper, portobello, garlic, olive oil, salt, and pepper. Toss until the vegetables are evenly coated with the oil. Transfer the vegetables to a large baking sheet, spread into a single layer, and roast for about 25 minutes.

4. Arrange the flatbreads on a large baking sheet. Spread about $1/4$ cup of béchamel sauce on each flatbread. Divide the roasted vegetables among the flatbreads. Sprinkle each one with $1/2$ cup Parmesan cheese. Bake the flatbreads for about 10 minutes, or until very hot.

5. Remove the flatbreads from the oven. Sprinkle the goat cheese and the feta cheese over the top of each. Top each flatbread with a little basil.

" Since I'm a big fan of béchamel sauce, I love this flatbread. It's a great dish for when you want to clean out the fridge and use up a lot of vegetables."

80

THE ULTIMATE BURGER

This burger is juicy and flavorful thanks to the combination of chuck and short ribs (fattier than chuck). When mixed together, the result is an ultimate burger. It's worth a trip to the butcher to get the meat freshly ground.

SERVES 6 | LEVEL: JUMP SHOT

2 pounds ground beef (60% short rib and 40% chuck)

1/4 large yellow onion, chopped

1–2 thinly sliced scallions

1 large egg

3 garlic cloves, finely chopped

Kosher salt and freshly ground black pepper to taste

2 tablespoons Chef Max's Spice Blend (page 41)

3 tablespoons mayonnaise

6 kaiser rolls

6 slices Muenster cheese

Pickle spears

1. Preheat an outdoor grill or an oven broiler to medium.

2. In a large mixing bowl, combine the ground beef, chopped onion, scallions, egg, garlic, salt, pepper, and Chef Max's Spice Blend. Mix well, using your hands.

3. Form the mixture into 6 patties, each about 1 1/2 inches thick. Grill the burgers for about 10 minutes or until done, turning once.

4. Spread the rolls with mayonnaise. When the burgers are cooked, remove them from the grill and transfer them to the rolls. Top each burger with a slice of cheese. Garnish each burger with a pickle.

82

It's always a good idea to use a meat thermometer to take the meat's temperature, but take care when you do this with burgers. It's all too easy to get a false reading if the thermometer goes right through the burger and touches the grill pan.

"This is one of my guilty
pleasures after a big workout.
I like to make these for my
kids on Chef's day off."

GRILLED VEGETABLE WRAPS

Another great place to "hide" vegetables, these are anything but boring. Consider doubling the pesto recipe and using leftovers on pasta or spread on bread.

SERVES 6 | LEVEL: JUMP SHOT

For the pesto:

1/4 cup feta cheese

1/4 cup oil-packed sun-dried tomatoes

2 tablespoons pine nuts

3 tablespoons extra-virgin olive oil

For the wraps:

2 zucchini, sliced

2 yellow summer squash, sliced 1/4-inch thick

1/2 large red onion, sliced 1/4-inch thick

1/2 red bell pepper, cored, seeded, and sliced 1/4-inch thick

1/2 orange bell pepper, cored, seeded, and sliced 1/4-inch thick

1/2 green bell pepper, cored, seeded, and sliced 1/4-inch thick

4 fresh basil leaves, sliced into chiffonade

1/4 cup extra-virgin olive oil

2 tablespoons balsamic vinegar

3 garlic cloves, minced

Kosher salt and freshly ground black pepper to taste

3 12-inch flour tortillas

1. Make the pesto: In the work bowl of a food processor, combine the feta cheese, sun-dried tomatoes, pine nuts, and olive oil. Puree the mixture until it is very smooth.

2. Make the wraps: Set a large grill pan over medium heat and preheat it for 2 minutes.

3. In a large bowl, toss the zucchini, summer squash, red onion, bell peppers, basil, olive oil, balsamic vinegar, garlic, salt, and pepper. Grill the vegetables for 4 to 5 minutes or until they soften and develop grill marks, turning once or twice as they cook. Remove the vegetables from the grill pan.

4. Place the tortillas on the grill pan for about 30 seconds or until they are hot and pliable. Remove the wraps from the grill pan and spread each with some of the pesto. Transfer some of the grilled vegetables to one end of each tortilla. Season with a little salt and pepper.

5. Fold the tortilla to enclose the filling, then fold over both edges of the tortilla. Continue to fold up the wrap tightly. Cut each wrap in half and serve.

> " This is a great way to get extra nutrients because it's so packed with vegetables. It's one of Alexis's favorite wraps. "

85

TUNA WRAPS WITH MANDARIN ORANGES AND SWEET CHILI SAUCE

Fresh ginger in the marinade and in the dipping sauce gives these wraps a pleasantly pungent and spicy flavor. Unpeeled fresh gingerroot can be wrapped tightly in plastic and stored in the refrigerator for up to 3 weeks, or you can freeze it for months.

SERVES 6 | LEVEL: JUMP SHOT

1 tablespoon soy sauce

1 tablespoon honey

1 teaspoon grated fresh ginger

1 tablespoon packed light brown sugar

1/2 teaspoon freshly ground black pepper

2 pounds sushi-grade tuna, cut into 24 slices

1/4 pound arugula

1 teaspoon sesame oil

6 rice noodle wraps

For the dipping sauce:

1/2 cup sweet chili sauce

1 teaspoon grated fresh ginger

1/4 cup canned mandarin oranges, drained

2 tablespoons chopped scallion (white and green parts)

1. In a medium bowl, combine the soy sauce, honey, ginger, brown sugar, and black pepper. Whisk until well blended. Place the tuna into this marinade, turn to coat well, and set it aside for 10 minutes.

2. In a small bowl, toss the arugula with the sesame oil.

3. Place the rice noodle wraps into a large baking pan, cover them with warm water, and let sit for 25 seconds, or until they are pliable.

4. Remove the wraps from the water and place them on a plate. Arrange some arugula on top of each wrap. Top each with 4 slices of the tuna. Spoon a teaspoon of the marinade over the tuna. Roll up the wrap tightly.

5. In a blender, puree the sweet chili sauce, ginger, mandarin oranges, and scallion. Transfer the dipping sauce to a ramekin. Serve the wrap with the dipping sauce.

BRIE AND MOZZARELLA SANDWICHES

The combination of two cheeses in one sandwich makes everyone happy. The bread should be sliced thick, as for Texas toast.

SERVES 4 TO 6 | LEVEL: JUMP SHOT

For the herb pesto:

2 tablespoons stemmed, chopped fresh cilantro

3 garlic cloves, peeled

2 tablespoons pine nuts

$\frac{1}{2}$ cup extra-virgin olive oil

$\frac{1}{4}$ cup freshly grated Parmesan cheese

Kosher salt and freshly ground black pepper to taste

For the sandwiches:

1 3-pound loaf of sourdough bread, sliced thick

1 pound fresh mozzarella cheese, sliced

1 pound Brie cheese, sliced

Extra-virgin olive oil, for brushing on the bread

1. Make the herb pesto: In the work bowl of a food processor, combine the cilantro, garlic, pine nuts, and olive oil. Puree the mixture until it is very smooth. Add the Parmesan cheese, salt, and pepper.

2. Preheat a large grill pan over medium heat for about 2 minutes.

3. Spread some of the herb pesto on each slice of bread. Make sandwiches, using the mozzarella and Brie.

4. Brush each sandwich with a little olive oil. Place the sandwiches in a single layer on the grill pan and grill for about 2 minutes per side or until the cheese melts. Cut into halves or quarters and serve immediately.

88

"I am a big fan of homemade mozzarella, especially after we visited a market and I saw it being made by hand. Brie happens to be Alexis's favorite cheese. This sandwich is a real winner."

ROASTED TURKEY AND CUCUMBER SANDWICHES

This is a great way to use up leftover turkey. Of course, you can leave out any vegetable you don't have, or add any vegetables that you like. Ciabatta (in Italian, this means "slipper") is a chubby loaf of bread that is soft inside and crusty on the outside. If you can't find it, use a large loaf of country white bread instead.

SERVES 4 | LEVEL: LAYUP

2 teaspoons unsalted butter

$^{1}/_{2}$ medium red onion, sliced thin

2 garlic cloves, minced

2 tablespoons sugar

3 tablespoons extra-virgin olive oil

8 slices ciabatta

$^{1}/_{4}$ cup mayonnaise

2 tablespoons Sriracha sauce

$^{1}/_{2}$ pound roasted turkey, sliced thin

$^{1}/_{2}$ pound Swiss cheese, sliced thin

1 ripe avocado, peeled, pitted, and sliced

$^{1}/_{2}$ English cucumber, sliced thin

$^{1}/_{4}$ pound sprouts

Gherkins, for garnish

Cherry tomatoes, for garnish

1. Set a 10-inch skillet over medium heat and let it preheat for about 30 seconds. Add the butter to the skillet, and when it melts, add the onion, garlic, and sugar. Cook, stirring, for about 5 minutes or until the onion is caramelized. Remove the onion and garlic to a plate. Allow the skillet to cool slightly. Wash and dry the skillet.

2. Return the skillet to the burner and heat the olive oil over medium heat for 30 seconds. Add the ciabatta slices and cook for 1 minute or until each one is golden, turning once. Remove the ciabatta from the skillet and set aside.

3. In a small bowl, whisk the mayonnaise and the Sriracha sauce. Set aside.

4. Arrange the slices of ciabatta on a large pan. Spread each slice with some mayonnaise. On top of half the slices, layer on turkey and cheese. Top with some avocado slices, cucumber slices, caramelized onion, and sprouts. Add a second slice of ciabatta to each sandwich. Press down firmly.

5. Slice each sandwich in half. Spear a gherkin and cherry tomato with a frilled toothpick and insert into each sandwich half as a garnish.

MINI FISH TACOS WITH CILANTRO CRÈME FRAÎCHE

These are fun to make and eat. Grouper is lean, firm, and easily available, but you can use just about whatever kind of firm white fish you like. By the way, any leftover mango salsa is delicious with chicken or fish.

MAKES 6 TACOS | LEVEL: JUMP SHOT

For the mango salsa:

2 large mangoes

1/4 cup chopped red onion

2 tablespoons stemmed, chopped fresh cilantro

2 tablespoons extra-virgin olive oil

1/2 jalapeño pepper, chopped

1/4 green bell pepper, cored, seeded, and diced

1 teaspoon agave nectar

Juice of 1 orange

Kosher salt and freshly ground black pepper to taste

For the tacos:

1 pound grouper fillet

2 tablespoons Chef Max's Spice Blend (page 41)

1 cup all-purpose flour

Kosher salt and freshly ground black pepper to taste

1/2 cup extra-virgin olive oil

1/4 cup crème fraîche or sour cream

4 tablespoons stemmed, chopped fresh cilantro

6 small corn tortillas

1/4 cup shredded purple cabbage

1 lime, cut into six wedges

1. Make the mango salsa: In a small bowl, toss mango, red onion, cilantro, olive oil, jalapeño pepper, bell pepper, agave nectar, orange juice, salt, and pepper. Cover and refrigerate for at least 30 minutes.

2. In a medium bowl, sprinkle the grouper with Chef Max's Spice Blend. Set aside.

3. Preheat a 10-inch sauté pan over medium heat for 1 minute. In a shallow bowl, season the flour with some salt and pepper. Dust the grouper with the

92

flour. Pour the olive oil into the sauté pan and when it sizzles, add the grouper. Sauté the grouper for about 3 minutes, or until done. Remove the grouper from the sauté pan and cut it into bite-sized chunks. Set aside.

4. In a small bowl, whisk the crème fraîche with half the cilantro and some salt and pepper.

5. Warm the corn tortillas in a small sauté pan for about 30 seconds or until they are soft and pliable. Set aside.

6. To make the tacos, place some grouper in the center of each tortilla. Add some shredded cabbage and mango salsa. Top with the crème fraîche and garnish with the remaining cilantro. Serve the lime wedges on the side.

"I developed a taste for Mexican food when we lived in Arizona, and Alexis likes it, too, so we make these often. They're the real deal."

94

SALMON CAKES WITH GARLIC AIOLI

Switch up this aioli, which is a garlic-flavored mayonnaise traditionally eaten with seafood or meat, by adding some fresh cilantro and capers. This is a great accompaniment to the salmon cakes, but you can also use it on other sandwiches.

SERVES 4 TO 6 | LEVEL: JUMP SHOT

For the garlic aioli:

2 garlic cloves, minced

1/4 cup mayonnaise

1 teaspoon capers, drained and rinsed

1 teaspoon stemmed, chopped fresh cilantro

1 teaspoon freshly squeezed lemon juice

Kosher salt and freshly ground black pepper to taste

For the salmon cakes:

2 cups diced salmon fillet, skinless and boneless

1/4 cup diced yellow onion

1 tablespoon stemmed, chopped fresh parsley

2 eggs, lightly beaten

2 tablespoons Grey Poupon mustard

1 cup dried bread crumbs

1/4 cup diced fresh pineapple

2 tablespoons mayonnaise

1 teaspoon minced fresh garlic

1 tablespoon chopped fresh dill

1/4 cup tricolor pepper, cored, seeded, and diced

1 teaspoon Cajun Seasoning

Kosher salt and freshly ground black pepper to taste

2 tablespoons all-purpose flour

1/4 cup extra-virgin olive oil, for frying

Lemon wedges, for garnish

1. Make the garlic aioli: In a small bowl, combine the garlic, mayonnaise, capers, cilantro, lemon juice, salt, and pepper. Cover and set aside while you prepare the salmon.

2. Make the salmon cakes: In a large bowl, combine the salmon, onion, parsley, eggs, mustard, bread crumbs, pineapple, mayonnaise, garlic, dill, tricolor pepper, Cajun Seasoning, salt, and pepper. Mix very well. Using your

95

hands, form the mixture into 3-inch patties. Lightly dust each salmon cake with a little flour.

3. In a large sauté pan, heat the oil over medium for 1 minute. Add the salmon cakes to the pan and cook for 2 to 3 minutes. Carefully flip the cakes and cook for an additional 3 to 4 minutes. Remove the cakes to a platter.

4. Serve the salmon cakes with the garlic aioli and garnish with the lemon wedges.

SALAD TRIO

This is easy to make in advance and keep in the refrigerator until you're ready to eat. It's tuna, egg, and chicken, but each one has a little twist to it. For the egg salad, pick up your favorite sweet relish at a local market.

SERVES 4 TO 6 | LEVEL: LAYUP

For the chicken salad:

$^1/_2$ cup mayonnaise

2 tablespoons stemmed, chopped cilantro

1 tablespoon curry powder

Kosher salt and freshly ground black pepper to taste

$^1/_4$ cup finely chopped yellow onion

2 teaspoons celery salt

3 whole chicken breasts, cooked and diced

2 tablespoons dried cranberries

For the tuna salad:

3 7-ounce cans water-packed tuna, drained and flaked

$^1/_2$ cup mayonnaise

1 tablespoon freshly squeezed lemon juice

1 tablespon Chef Max's Spice Blend (page 41)

Kosher salt and freshly ground black pepper to taste

For the egg salad:

8 large hard-boiled eggs, chopped

$^1/_2$ cup mayonnaise

3 tablespoons sweet relish

4 tablespoons finely chopped red onion

$^1/_2$ teaspoon white pepper

1 tablespoon yellow ball park mustard

1 teaspoon celery salt

1. Make the chicken salad: In a large bowl, combine the mayonnaise, cilantro, curry powder, salt, pepper, onion, and celery salt. Add the diced chicken and the dried cranberries, and stir to combine. Cover and refrigerate.

2. Make the tuna salad: In a large bowl, combine the tuna, mayonnaise, lemon juice, Chef Max's Spice Blend, salt, and pepper. Stir well. Cover and refrigerate.

97

3. Make the egg salad: In a large bowl, combine the eggs, mayonnaise, relish, red onion, white pepper, mustard, and celery salt. Stir to combine. Cover and refrigerate.

4. Arrange a scoop of each of the salads on your choice of greens.

CALIFORNIA COBB SALAD

A California garden inspired this dish, which features plenty of fresh vegetables as well as turkey bacon rather than regular bacon. Swap in other greens if you like, as this salad is fairly easy to customize.

SERVES 6 | LEVEL: LAYUP

For the salad:

1 head romaine lettuce, washed, dried, and chopped

1 head butter lettuce, washed, dried, and chopped

8 strips turkey bacon, cooked and diced

1 avocado, peeled, pitted, and diced

4 hard-boiled eggs, cut in half lengthwise

$^{1}/_{4}$ cup finely diced red onion

$^{1}/_{4}$ cup finely diced green bell pepper

$^{1}/_{4}$ cup crumbled blue cheese

$^{1}/_{4}$ cup chopped scallion

For the tangy cilantro vinaigrette:

$^{1}/_{2}$ bunch cilantro, stemmed

2 garlic cloves, minced

$^{1}/_{2}$ shallot, chopped

$^{1}/_{4}$ cup Champagne vinegar

2 tablespoons honey

1 tablespoon Dijon mustard

$^{1}/_{2}$ cup extra-virgin olive oil

$^{1}/_{4}$ teaspoon freshly ground black pepper

1. Arrange the romaine and butter lettuce on a large, rectangular platter.

2. Working from left to right, arrange the other salad ingredients in straight rows over the lettuce. You should have a row of diced bacon, 1 of avocado, 1 of hard-boiled egg, 1 of red onion, 1 of bell pepper, 1 of blue cheese, and 1 of scallion. Cover the salad, and refrigerate until ready to serve.

3. To make the tangy cilantro vinaigrette: In a blender or a food processor, combine the cilantro, garlic, shallot, Champagne vinegar, honey, and Dijon mustard. Blend well. With the blender running, slowly add the olive oil and blend for 30 seconds or until the dressing is thick and creamy. Stir in the pepper. When ready to serve, pour the dressing over the salad.

99

COOKING WITH AMAR'E

"I like this salad, which I can easily make for my family and friends. It has a wide array of ingredients and looks great when plated, which makes me look like a true chef! Occasionally, Chef makes this salad for me to eat as a pregame snack or when I'm running out the door headed to an event."

TEAM DINNER

....

BRAISED BARBECUED BEEF RIBS 109

GARLIC AND HERB–INFUSED PRIME RIB 113

BLACKENED FLANK STEAK WITH
CHIMICHURRI AND GRILLED PINEAPPLE 115

GRILLED NEW YORK STRIP STEAK WITH
HORSERADISH CREAM AND SAUTÉED MUSHROOMS 119

LOADED BEEF STEW 122

STAT STEAK 124

GRILLED VEAL CHOPS WITH PEACH AND APPLE CHUTNEY 125

ROSEMARY AND GARLIC LEG OF LAMB 128

GRILLED LAMB CHOPS WITH TZATZIKI 130

GRILLED CHICKEN BREAST WITH COUSCOUS PILAF 133

ROASTED CHICKEN WITH
GARLIC AND CILANTRO HONEY GLAZE 135

JERK CHICKEN 137

GRILLED CORNISH HENS WITH CITRUS AND HONEY GLAZE 139

CARRIBEAN PAN-SEARED SNAPPER ESCOVITCH 140

PAN-ROASTED SALMON WITH FRESH TOMATO SALSA 142

ALMOND-CRUSTED SOLE WITH
GINGER-LIME BEURRE BLANC 144

HERB-CRUSTED SEA BASS WITH
CHAMPAGNE CURRY CREAM 147

PAN-SEARED BAY SCALLOPS WITH ARUGULA SALAD 149

PAELLA 151

SALMON PINWHEELS WITH GARLIC HERB CREAM CHEESE 153

COCONUT AND CORN SALAD 154

TOMATO AND RADISH SLAW 157

ICEBERG WEDGE WITH BUTTERMILK BLUE CHEESE DRESSING,
CANDIED TEARDROP TOMATOES, SHAVED ONIONS,
CHIVES, AND EGGS 158

CUCUMBER AND TOMATO SALAD 160

GRILLED CABBAGE WITH BALSAMIC BUTTER 161

STEWED OKRA 162

ENTERTAINING

AMAR'E

When I was growing up, my aunt cooked dinner often for my family. I loved eating her food, because she cooked from her soul. Our family bonded over her delicious meals. Her sautéed steak was always seasoned just right, and she made the best meatloaf. It was very flavorful and moist, and she basted it with one of my favorite condiments (well, at the time one of my favorite foods), ketchup. On Sundays, everyone would come over just to eat her meatloaf.

There's almost nothing I like eating better than a good meatloaf, some steak, or some ribs. Comfort foods like these make me happy and please my stomach. But even though I have always loved to eat, I sure didn't know the first thing about cooking. The older guys in my family did the cooking. I just showed up with a basketball in my hands and a hungry belly after playing all day. I was too busy shooting hoops to learn how to cook. I just wanted to eat!

But once I had kids of my own, I wanted to cook for them. Before I met Chef, I would get in the kitchen on my days off and try to make them breakfast. Sometimes I would try to grill some hot dogs and hamburgers for them as well. Hamburger Helper was a staple before I hooked up with Chef.

Of course, I really didn't know what I was doing in the kitchen. I didn't know the meaning of *sauté*, had trouble understanding the different marinades and what they were for, and was familiar with just one cooking technique: frying!

Since Chef has been teaching me to cook, I've become an expert at chopping vegetables and cutting up meat. I love to grill and I can cook just about anything on the grill. The burgers and hot dogs that I make for my kids now aren't burned to a crisp the way that I once made them. (And it's been a while since I made Hamburger Helper.)

Now dinner is a time for us all to come together as a family. We are avid readers in our house, so there is always some discussion about the books we're reading. It's when we catch up on the day and have some really fun conversations with our children. And of course, there's the food. In this chapter are all the great recipes we enjoy eating for dinner, and that I have learned to cook for my family.

MAX "

Amar'e really wanted to cook dinner for his family, but he wasn't sure how to go about it. The one time that I remember him trying to make steaks, he put them on the grill when it was still cold. That meat wound up tasting and smelling like the grill itself. Whenever he tried making steaks and burgers, he overcooked them.

But then one day, when I was putting steaks on the grill, I showed Amar'e how to season the rib eye with rosemary, garlic, and thyme. Just for the record, I think that everyone should know how to prepare the rib eye, which is the most flavorful cut of meat and a dinner party favorite for Amar'e. Next, we made a beef stew together, with lots of root vegetables. Amar'e was really interested, an eager student.

Since his teammates love my Grilled Lamb Chops with Tzatziki (page 130), Amar'e and I worked together until he made chops that looked and tasted exactly like mine. Amar'e loves a nice roasted chicken and Southern fried chicken, so he wanted to learn how to make both. After some sessions in the kitchen together, he mastered a variety of chicken dishes.

I wanted Amar'e to learn a lot of different cooking techniques so that he could feel comfortable in the kitchen when making dinner. Grilling, baking, roasting, and pan-searing are all important cooking methods that he's learning to perfect.

Now he entertains his friends on my day off, making them prime rib (Garlic and Herb–Infused Prime Rib, page 113) and grilled lamb chops. On Sundays, when he and his wife and kids have a nice family dinner, he can even cook a leg of lamb (Rosemary and Garlic Leg of Lamb, page 128).

Since he began learning to cook, Amar'e's tastes have changed. He really understands the different flavors of herbs and spices and what they go with. He's much more comfortable in the kitchen than he was, and it shows in his cooking.

THE POINTS GAME

Dinner at our house is about a lot more than
the food. It's a time when we share our day's
experiences, both good and not so good.
Everyone gets the chance to talk about what
they did and what they were proud of. It's a time
when Alexis and I encourage the kids to share
their feelings and to grow closer to one another.

Each night we start out the meal by asking the kids about their day. If there is
something that bothered them, we want to hear about it. We ask each of the kids
what was their favorite moment, and then we focus specifically on what each of them
learned. It's our intent to teach our kids how important it is to learn new things each
and every day.

Next, we play a game called the Points Game. I ask them random trivia questions
that can be on just about any subject. That's what makes it so much fun! Each time
a child answers a question correctly, he or she gets a point. And at the end of the
game, whoever has the most points wins the game. So it's a little competitive—but in a
positive way. Everyone has a good time and we share a lot of laughs. We always look
forward to sitting down together at our table each night.

BRAISED BARBECUED BEEF RIBS

You can prepare these ahead of time so they are ready when your guests come over. Leftovers are delicious in quesadillas or in a nice grilled cheese sandwich. Sweet Baby Ray barbecue sauce is widely available but you can also make your own (Barbecue Sauce, page 32).

SERVES 6 TO 8 | LEVEL: JUMP SHOT

6 bone-in short ribs (about 5¾ pounds)

Kosher salt

Extra-virgin olive oil

1 large Spanish onion, chopped into ½-inch pieces

2 celery stalks, chopped into ½-inch pieces

2 carrots, cut in half lengthwise, and chopped into ½-inch pieces

2 garlic cloves, smashed

½ bunch fresh cilantro, stemmed and chopped

1 6-ounce can tomato paste

1 cup hearty red wine

1 cup Vegetable Stock, plus more as needed (page 24)

½ cup Sweet Baby Ray barbecue sauce

1 bunch fresh thyme, tied with kitchen string

2 bay leaves

2 lemons, sliced into rings

1. Season each short rib generously with salt. Coat a very large stockpot with olive oil. If you don't have a pot large enough to hold all the meat and vegetables, divide them between two pots. Set the pot over high heat.

2. Add the short ribs to the pot and brown them very well, about 2 to 3 minutes per side. Do not overcrowd the pan. Cook in batches, if necessary.

3. Preheat the oven to 375°F.

4. While the short ribs are browning, puree the onion, celery, carrots, garlic, and cilantro in a food processor until a coarse paste forms.

109

5. When the short ribs are very brown on all sides, remove them from the pan. Pour off the fat into a small, heatproof bowl. (You can dispose of it when it cools down.) Coat the bottom of the same pan with about $\frac{1}{4}$ cup of additional oil and add the pureed vegetables. Season the vegetables generously with salt and brown them on medium-low for 5 to 7 minutes, or until they are softened.

6. Add the tomato paste. Cook over medium heat for 3 to 4 minutes. Add the wine and vegetable stock, and cook, scraping the bottom of the pan, for about 10 minutes or until the liquid is reduced by half. Lower the heat if the mixture starts to burn.

7. Return the short ribs to the pan and add the barbecue sauce. Add the thyme bundle and the bay leaves.

8. Cover the pan and bake for 2 hours, checking periodically and adding more stock if the meat seems to be drying out. Turn the ribs over after 90 minutes. Remove the lid during the last 20 minutes of cooking so the meat gets nice and brown and the sauce is reduced. When the meat is very tender but not falling apart, remove it from the oven. Remove the bay leaves. Serve it with the braising liquid. Garnish with lemon slices.

"One of my winning post-game favorites. If Chef is off for the evening, I prep this before the game or practice and have an amazing dish when we return home afterward."

111

WHISK
(AND DRIBBLE!)
WITH EASE

There are many reasons to make homemade salad dressing or vinaigrette. It tastes fresher than a bottled dressing, it costs less, and chances are good that you already have the ingredients right in your pantry. Once you learn the basic formula, you won't even really need to use a recipe. It's easier to make this basic recipe than it is to do a layup!

Plan on one part vinegar (or another acidic ingredient like lemon juice) to every three parts oil. In a container, dissolve a little salt in the vinegar. Whisk in a teaspoon of Dijon mustard, if you like, along with some finely minced fresh herbs. Very finely minced shallots or garlic are other possible additions.

Now whisk in the oil gradually, pouring it in a very thin stream. Taste and add extra salt and a little freshly ground black pepper before drizzling, or dribbling, over your favorite greens.

GARLIC AND HERB-INFUSED PRIME RIB

Roasting the meat at a high temperature for a brief period sears it and locks in all the flavors. Serve this with horseradish cream, garlic mashed potatoes, and Brussels sprouts.

SERVES 6 TO 8 | LEVEL: JUMP SHOT

5 garlic cloves, chopped

4 sprigs fresh rosemary, chopped

4 sprigs fresh thyme, chopped

3 teaspoons freshly ground black pepper

4 teaspoons kosher salt

3 tablespoons extra-virgin olive oil

3 teaspoons Chef Max's Spice Blend (page 41)

1 4-bone dry-aged prime rib (about 5 pounds)

1 large yellow onion, chopped

2 carrots, diced

2 celery stalks, diced

1 leek, chopped

1. In a medium bowl, combine the garlic, rosemary, thyme, black pepper, salt, olive oil, and Chef Max's Spice Blend. Rub this mixture on both sides as well as the ends of the prime rib. Place the meat into a large glass baking pan, cover it with plastic wrap, and allow it to marinate in the refrigerator for at least 1 hour, or as long as overnight.

2. An hour before you plan to cook the meat, remove it from the refrigerator. About 20 minutes before you plan to cook the meat, preheat the oven to 400°F.

3. In a roasting pan large enough to hold the prime rib, arrange the onion, carrots, celery, and leek. Place the meat on top of the vegetables. Roast the meat for 30 minutes. Reduce the oven heat to 350°F and continue to roast the meat for another 90 minutes, basting every 30 minutes with the pan juices and any drippings from the bottom of the roasting pan.

113

4. Remove the meat when it is medium-rare, which is when the internal temperature of the meat reaches 130°F to 135°F. To check the temperature, insert a meat thermometer into the center of the meat. Let the meat roast for an additional 10 to 15 minutes if you would like it more well-done.

5. When the meat has reached the desired doneness, remove it from the oven and allow it to rest for 15 to 20 minutes before slicing. Slice it into $1/2$-inch-thick slices.

"This is a Knicks' favorite. I make it when I have friends over, and it's a great dish for company."

BLACKENED FLANK STEAK WITH CHIMICHURRI AND GRILLED PINEAPPLE

This is a great barbecue dish to make in the summer; slicing the steak against the grain will ensure maximum tenderness.

SERVES 6 TO 8 | LEVEL: JUMP SHOT

2 teaspoons garlic powder

2 teaspoons onion powder

3 teaspoons sugar

2 teaspoons mild paprika

2 teaspoons chili powder

1 teaspoon kosher salt

1 teaspoon freshly ground black pepper

1 teaspoon cayenne pepper

$1/2$ teaspoon mustard powder

1 teaspoon dried oregano

1 teaspoon dried thyme

1 2-pound flank steak

Grilled Pineapple (recipe follows)

Chimichurri (recipe follows)

1. In a small bowl, combine the garlic powder, onion powder, sugar, paprika, chili powder, salt, black pepper, cayenne pepper, mustard powder, oregano, and thyme.

2. Rub this all over the flank steak. Allow the steak to rest at room temperature for about 1 hour.

3. Heat a 12-inch nonstick grill pan or a cast-iron skillet over medium-high heat for about 3 minutes. Place the steak on the grill pan, and cook for about 3 minutes per side, or until done to your liking.

4. Remove the steak from the pan and allow it to rest for 15 to 20 minutes. Slice it horizontally, across the grain, into $1/2$-inch slices. Serve the steak with Chimichurri and Grilled Pineapple.

116

CHIMICHURRI

Chimichurri is a thick parsley-and-olive-oil-based sauce that's a must with grilled meats, steak, and chicken. It's always good to have chimichurri in the fridge, ready to go.

SERVES 6 | LEVEL: LAYUP

½ bunch cilantro, stemmed

½ bunch parsley, stemmed

2 cloves garlic, peeled

2 tablespoons red wine vinegar

¼ cup extra-virgin olive oil

1 teaspoon red pepper flakes

Kosher salt and freshly ground black pepper to taste

1. In the work bowl of a food processor, combine the cilantro, parsley, garlic, red wine vinegar, olive oil, red pepper flakes, salt, and black pepper.

2. Pulse the mixture until it is smooth. Transfer the chimichurri to a serving bowl and set it aside for about 30 minutes to let the flavors develop.

GRILLED PINEAPPLE

Leaving the rings whole rather than cutting out the center core ensures that they don't dry out. Serve the pineapple with grilled chicken and other grilled dishes.

SERVES 8 OR MORE | LEVEL: LAYUP

2 large ripe pineapples

1/2 bunch cilantro, stemmed

1/4 cup extra-virgin olive oil

Kosher salt and freshly ground black pepper to taste

1. Trim away all the sharp points of the pineapple tuft, then hold the tuft firmly in one hand and carefully remove the pineapple skin with a sharp knife by cutting down through the fruit. Remove the pineapple "eyes" with the sharp point of the knife. Slice off the pineapple tuft. Slice the pineapple into 1-inch thick rings.

2. In a large mixing bowl, combine the cilantro, olive oil, salt, and pepper. Add the pineapple rings. Allow the pineapple rings to marinate in the mixture for anywhere from 30 minutes to overnight.

3. Preheat the grill to medium-high. Remove the pineapple from the marinade and allow any excess marinade to drip off. Place the pineapple rings on the grill and grill for about 2 minutes, turning once halfway through the cooking. Remove the pineapple rings from the grill when they have visible grill marks and have softened and are nicely browned.

118

GRILLED NEW YORK STRIP STEAK WITH HORSERADISH CREAM AND SAUTÉED MUSHROOMS

You want to look for meat with a lot of marbling, so it has a good fat content. Or you can be a big shot and buy Kobe beef! This steak is delicious with the horseradish cream.

SERVES 6 TO 8 | LEVEL: JUMP SHOT

¹/₂ cup sour cream

2 tablespoons prepared horseradish

2 teaspoons Worcestershire sauce

¹/₂ teaspoon white pepper

Kosher salt to taste

2 cloves garlic, minced

1 sprig fresh thyme, chopped

2 tablespoons extra-virgin olive oil

1 teaspoon Chef Max's Spice Blend (page 41)

Freshly ground black pepper to taste

6 8-ounce aged New York strip steaks

Sautéed Mushrooms (recipe follows)

1. Make the horseradish cream: In a small mixing bowl, combine the sour cream, horseradish, Worcestershire sauce, white pepper, and salt. Cover and refrigerate.

2. In a large mixing bowl, combine the garlic, thyme, olive oil, Chef Max's Spice Blend, salt, and pepper.

3. Rub this mixture all over the steaks, then wrap the steaks tightly in plastic wrap. Refrigerate them for at least 30 minutes.

4. Preheat the grill to medium-high. Remove the steaks from the refrigerator, unwrap them, and place them on the grill. Grill the steaks for about 3 minutes per side, or until they reach the desired doneness (130°F to 135°F for medium-rare).

5. Serve the steaks with Sautéed Mushrooms and garnish with the horseradish cream.

119

SAUTÉED MUSHROOMS

Serve this as a good side dish for dinner; it tastes great with just about any kind of roast.

SERVES 4 TO 6 | LEVEL: LAYUP

2 tablespoons unsalted butter

2 cloves garlic, minced

2 shallots, thinly sliced

1 pound button mushrooms, wiped clean and sliced

1 sprig thyme, chopped

$1/4$ cup white wine

Kosher salt and freshly ground black pepper to taste

1. Preheat a 12-inch sauté pan over medium heat for 2 minutes. Add the butter and let it melt.

2. Add the garlic and shallot to the pan. Cook over medium heat for 1 minute. Add the mushrooms, thyme, and wine, and cook for 2 minutes. Remove from the heat and season with salt and pepper. Serve immediately.

LOADED BEEF STEW

This stew is "loaded" because of all the great root vegetables in it. This is a perfect make-ahead dish that tastes even better on the second day. When making this stew, you'll prepare a roux, a mixture of flour and oil that is cooked and added to sauces to thicken them. Leftover roux will keep in the refrigerator, covered, for a few weeks. We like to serve this stew in large bowls with slices of corn bread.

SERVES 6 TO 8 | LEVEL: LAYUP

1 bay leaf

3 pounds beef top round, cut into
  1-inch chunks

1¼ cups extra-virgin olive oil

5 garlic cloves, chopped

4 cups beef stock

¼ cup tomato paste

1 large yellow onion, chopped

2 celery stalks, chopped

2 sprigs fresh thyme, finely chopped

3 tablespoons Chef Max's Spice Blend
  (page 41)

1 cup red wine

1 cup all-purpose flour

1 yam, peeled and diced

2 parsnips, peeled and chopped

1 rutabaga, peeled and chopped

1 red or green bell pepper, cored,
  seeded, and chopped

3½ pound baby carrots

1 plantain, peeled and chopped

¼ head cabbage, sliced

1 bunch cilantro, stemmed

Kosher salt and freshly ground black
  pepper to taste

1. In a 10-quart stockpot, bring 4 cups of water, the bay leaf, and the beef to a boil. Reduce to a simmer and cook, covered, for 45 minutes. Pour off the water. Add ¼ cup of the olive oil and the garlic. Sauté for 2 to 3 minutes.

2. Add the beef stock, tomato paste, onion, celery, thyme, Chef Max's Spice Blend, and red wine. Bring to a boil and simmer, covered, for 45 minutes, stirring occasionally.

3. While the stew is simmering, make the roux by combining the remaining cup of olive oil and the flour in a small, heavy saucepan. Turn the heat to medium and cook, stirring, until it is smooth and light brown. Measure out $\frac{1}{4}$ cup of roux and refrigerate the rest.

4. Add the yam, parsnip, rutabaga, bell pepper, carrot, plantain, cabbage, cilantro, and $\frac{1}{4}$ cup roux to the stew. Stir very well. Sprinkle with salt and pepper. Simmer the stew, covered, for about 1 hour or until the vegetables and the meat are tender.

STAT STEAK

A great Sunday night supper, this juicy, tender steak is delicious with potatoes au gratin and Brussels sprouts. Be sure to buy steaks that are all about the same size so they will cook evenly.

SERVES 6 | LEVEL: LAYUP

For the rub:

1/4 cup packed light brown sugar

1/2 cup garlic powder

1/2 cup onion powder

2 tablespoons sea salt

1/4 cup paprika

3 tablespoons chopped fresh thyme

1/4 cup freshly ground black pepper

For the steaks:

6 10-ounce rib eye steaks

1 garlic clove, minced

1 tablespoon olive oil

1 tablespoon Herb Butter (page 31), softened

1. Preheat the oven to 500°F or set the oven on the broil setting.

2. Prepare the rub: In a small bowl, combine the brown sugar, garlic powder, onion powder, sea salt, paprika, thyme, and black pepper.

3. Arrange the steaks on a large sheet pan or baking sheet. Season each steak on both sides with some of the rub.

4. Rub each steak with garlic and olive oil. Bake or broil the steaks for about 4 minutes per side. The steaks should have a nice char on both sides. Remove the steaks from the oven and top with a little Herb Butter. Return the steaks to the oven for 3 minutes or until they reach the desired degree of doneness.

GRILLED VEAL CHOPS WITH PEACH AND APPLE CHUTNEY

Definitely make the fruit chutney that goes with these chops, since it really brings out their flavor. You can have it ready in just a few minutes, and it's very simple to prepare.

SERVES 6 TO 8 | LEVEL: SLAM DUNK

3 10-ounce veal chops (about 1 1/2 inches thick)

Juice of 1/2 orange

Juice of 1/2 lime

Juice of 1/2 lemon

3 garlic cloves, minced

3 sprigs fresh mint

1/2 bunch cilantro, stemmed

2 tablespoons extra-virgin olive oil

3 teaspoons Chef Max's Spice Blend (page 41)

Kosher salt to taste

2 teaspoons freshly ground black pepper

Peach and Apple Chutney (recipe follows)

1. Arrange the veal chops in a large glass baking dish.

2. In a medium glass bowl, combine the orange juice, lime juice, lemon juice, garlic, mint, cilantro, olive oil, Chef Max's Spice Blend, salt, and pepper. Pour the marinade over the chops. Set the chops aside to marinate for at least 30 minutes or as long as overnight.

4. Preheat an outdoor grill to medium for about 15 minutes. Arrange the chops diagonally on the grill so that grill marks will form during the cooking. Grill the chops for about 3 minutes. Turn and grill on the other side for about 3 minutes or until medium-rare, or continue grilling them for a few minutes longer if you prefer your chops a little more well-done.

5. Transfer the chops to a large platter and serve with the Peach and Apple Chutney.

PEACH AND APPLE CHUTNEY

This is delicious with a variety of meats, and you could also eat it in a sandwich. Make this chutney ahead of time and store it in the refrigerator, tightly covered, for up to 5 days.

SERVES 6 | LEVEL: LAYUP

2 apples, peeled and sliced

2 peaches, peeled and sliced

1 shallot, thinly sliced

2 teaspoons unsalted butter

1/2 cup packed light brown sugar

1 teaspoon ground allspice

Kosher salt and freshly ground
 black pepper to taste

3 ounces Grand Marnier

1. Place a medium sauté pan over medium heat for 1 minute. In the sauté pan, combine the apple slices, peach slices, shallot, and butter.

2. Cook over medium heat, stirring, for 5 minutes or until the fruit is caramelized. It will soften and become golden brown.

3. Add the brown sugar, allspice, salt, and pepper. Stir in the Grand Marnier and continue to cook until the fruit is softened.

126

ROSEMARY AND GARLIC LEG OF LAMB

This dish tastes even better the second day, so make it ahead of time if you like. This is a classic leg of lamb with a good dose of fresh herbs. Serve this with a bottle of red wine for a perfect meal.

SERVES 6 TO 8 | LEVEL: JUMP SHOT

1 5-pound leg of lamb, at room temperature

4 garlic cloves, sliced into slivers

2 tablespoons Dijon mustard

1 tablespoon chopped fresh rosemary

1 tablespoon chopped fresh mint

1 tablespoon chopped fresh thyme

2 tablespoons Chef Max's Spice Blend (page 41)

1/2 cup red wine

1 lemon, halved

1 cup beef stock

3 shallots, chopped

2 carrots, diced

2 celery stalks, diced

Kosher salt and freshly ground black pepper to taste

1. Preheat the oven to 350°F.

2. Place the leg of lamb into a large roasting pan. With the tip of a sharp knife, cut 4 to 6 small slits in the leg of lamb, and insert the garlic slivers into the slits.

3. In a medium bowl, combine the Dijon mustard, rosemary, mint, thyme, Chef Max's Spice Blend, and red wine. Pour over the lamb in the roasting pan. Squeeze the lemon juice onto the lamb, and pour on the beef stock.

4. Arrange the shallots, carrots, and celery around the lamb. Sprinkle with salt and pepper.

5. Cover the roasting pan with foil. Bake the lamb for 1 hour and 15 minutes, or until it reaches an internal temperature of 130°F (for medium-rare). If you prefer more well-done meat, cook for 5 to 10 minutes more.

128

GRILLED LAMB CHOPS WITH TZATZIKI

Lamb is usually reserved for special occasions. In this recipe, the marinade really brings out the flavor in the chops. If you can, try to find lamb that is imported from New Zealand, which is always top quality, although you could certainly use domestic lamb as well with good results. Choose either loin lamb chops or rib lamb chops for this dish, and don't worry if you don't have a grill available. These chops may also be broiled in the oven, in which case you should add on about 5 minutes per side for medium. Serve them with the delicious Greek sauce called tzatziki, which is made with yogurt, garlic, and grated cucumber.

SERVES 6 TO 8　|　LEVEL: JUMP SHOT

For the chops:

1/4 cup balsamic vinegar

2 teaspoons finely chopped, fresh rosemary

3 teaspoons finely chopped garlic

1 cup extra-virgin olive oil

2 shallots, minced

3 sprigs fresh mint

Kosher salt and freshly ground black pepper to taste

3 pounds New Zealand lamb chops

For the tzatziki:

1 small cucumber, unpeeled, grated

1 garlic clove, minced

1 bunch fresh dill, stemmed and chopped

Zest of 1 lemon

1 cup Greek yogurt (low-fat, if preferred)

Kosher salt and freshly ground black pepper to taste

1. Prepare the chops: In a medium bowl, combine the balsamic vinegar, rosemary, garlic, olive oil, shallots, mint, and salt and pepper to taste.

2. Pour the mixture over the lamb chops in a large bowl, toss to coat, and marinate in the refrigerator for 2 hours.

3. Prepare the tzatziki: In a small bowl, combine the cucumber, garlic, dill, lemon zest, yogurt, and salt and pepper. Refrigerate for at least 30 minutes.

130

4. Preheat an outdoor grill to medium-high heat.

5. Remove the chops from the marinade. Brush them with any remaining marinade. Grill them to desired doneness, about 3 minutes per side for medium. Serve the chops with the tzatziki.

"A party isn't a party without lamb chops, and when we entertain at the house, I get in there with Chef and get some lamb chops going. I'm the grill guy on this dish."

GRILLED CHICKEN BREAST WITH COUSCOUS PILAF

Amar'e and I make this great dish together. I'll do the couscous while he does the chicken. It's an especially nice meal to serve in the summer.

SERVES 6 | LEVEL: JUMP SHOT

For the chicken:

6 boneless, skinless chicken breasts

Kosher salt and freshly ground black pepper to taste

1 teaspoon onion powder

1 teaspoon garlic powder

1 teaspoon mild paprika

1 teaspoon stemmed chopped fresh oregano

1 lemon, cut into wedges

For the couscous pilaf:

3 cups Chicken Stock (page 27)

$1\frac{1}{2}$ tablespoons unsalted butter

2 carrots, chopped

1 celery stalk, chopped

1 medium yellow onion, chopped

$1\frac{1}{2}$ cups couscous

1. Preheat a grill or a grill pan to medium heat.

2. Season the chicken breasts on both sides with the salt, pepper, onion powder, garlic powder, paprika, and oregano.

3. Grill the chicken for about 6 minutes or until it is done, flipping once. Remove the chicken to a platter. Grill the lemon wedges for 2 minutes or until grill marks appear. Set aside.

4. Make the couscous pilaf: In a large saucepan, bring the chicken stock and the butter to a boil over high heat. Add the carrots, celery, and onion, then cover and reduce the heat to medium-low. Cook for 5 minutes, or until the vegetables are tender. Stir in the couscous and simmer, covered, for about 10 minutes, or until all the liquid is absorbed. Fluff with a fork.

5. Place a large scoop of the couscous pilaf in the center of each plate. Place a chicken breast on top of the couscous. Garnish with the grilled lemon wedges.

133

ROASTED CHICKEN WITH GARLIC AND CILANTRO HONEY GLAZE

This straightforward dish doesn't require a huge number of ingredients. Though the marinade is best when made with fresh herbs, you can sub in dried rosemary and dried thyme in a pinch. Just use a teaspoon of dried rosemary and $3/4$ teaspoon of dried thyme. The glaze, which you can make ahead of time, really livens up a plain roasted chicken, too.

SERVES 6 TO 8 | LEVEL: JUMP SHOT

$1/4$ cup stemmed, chopped fresh cilantro

3 garlic cloves, minced

3 teaspoons chopped fresh rosemary

2 teaspoons chopped fresh thyme

$1/2$ cup extra-virgin olive oil

Kosher salt and freshly ground black pepper to taste

$1/4$ cup freshly squeezed lemon juice

2 teaspoons ground cumin

2 2- to 3-pound chickens, cut into quarters

1 cup white wine

For the garlic and cilantro honey glaze:

$1/4$ cup honey

2 garlic cloves, minced

$1/4$ cup orange juice

2 tablespoons stemmed, chopped cilantro

1. Make the chicken: In a small bowl, combine the cilantro, garlic, rosemary, thyme, $1/4$ cup of the olive oil, salt and pepper, lemon juice, and cumin. Place the chicken into a large bowl. Pour the marinade over the chicken. Using two large spoons, turn over the chicken pieces several times until they are well coated with the marinade. Allow to marinate for at least 30 minutes or overnight.

2. Preheat the oven to 375°F.

3. Preheat a large, ovenproof sauté pan over medium-high heat for 1 minute. Add the remaining $1/4$ cup olive oil and sear the chicken for 3 minutes on

135

each side. You may need to do this in several batches. Place the chicken into a large baking dish. Pour the white wine over the chicken.

4. Bake the chicken for 30 minutes or until it reaches 165°F.

5. Make the glaze: In a small bowl, whisk the honey, garlic, orange juice, and cilantro until well combined. Brush the cooked chicken with the glaze.

" We can't go wrong with an amazing chicken recipe. Chef Max and I came up with an easy, flavorful dish that I really enjoy. Have fun with the family when you make them this recipe."

JERK CHICKEN

The big difference between jerk chicken in the United States and in Jamaica is that in Jamaica, palmetto wood is used for the grilling. Still, you can use mesquite in this recipe with very good results. This chicken is spicy without being overwhelming, and perfectly crisp on the outside and juicy inside.

SERVES 6 TO 8 | LEVEL: JUMP SHOT

2 teaspoons ground allspice

$^1/_2$ teaspoon ground cinnamon

$^1/_2$ teaspoon ground nutmeg

$^1/_2$ large yellow onion, minced

8 garlic cloves, minced (or use 1 whole head of garlic)

1 teaspoon minced fresh ginger

3 scallions, sliced

Juice of 3 limes

$^1/_4$ cup low-sodium soy sauce

$^1/_4$ cup extra-virgin olive oil, plus more for drizzling

Kosher salt and freshly ground black pepper to taste

6 sprigs fresh thyme, chopped

1 Scotch bonnet pepper, halved (add more to taste if you like)

$^1/_4$ cup packed light brown sugar

2 whole free-range chickens (2 to 3 pounds each), cut into quarters

Lime wedges and parsley sprigs, for garnish, optional

1. Prepare the jerk marinade: In a blender, combine the allspice, cinnamon, nutmeg, onion, garlic, ginger, scallions, lime juice, soy sauce, olive oil, salt and pepper, thyme, Scotch bonnet pepper, and brown sugar. Process until the mixture becomes a smooth paste.

2. Place the chicken in a large resealable plastic bag. Pour in the marinade and seal the bag. Place it in a baking dish and refrigerate overnight.

3. Preheat the grill until the coals are gray. Add some mesquite chips, if you like. Grill the chicken, turning occasionally, for 20 minutes on each side.

137

4. Preheat the oven to 300°F. Transfer the chicken pieces to a baking sheet and drizzle with some olive oil. Bake in the oven "low and slow" until the chicken is tender, about 1 hour. The internal temperature of the chicken should be 165°F. Remove the chicken from the baking sheet to a serving platter, and garnish the platter with lime wedges and parsley sprigs, if using.

> "Jamaica, mon! I took my STAT (Stand Tall and Talented) team to Jamaica for vacation, and Chef and I found the real deal—an authentic jerk restaurant. After that experience, I was hooked on this great summer dish. Invite us over!"

138

GRILLED CORNISH HENS WITH CITRUS AND HONEY GLAZE

This is a great dish for entertaining. If you don't have Cornish hens, use this delicious glaze to liven up chicken or fish instead.

SERVES 8 | LEVEL: JUMP SHOT

For the Cornish hens:

4 Cornish hens, halved

3 tablespoons extra-virgin olive oil

Kosher salt and freshly ground black pepper to taste

Mild paprika to taste

4 lemons, halved

8 sprigs fresh rosemary

For the citrus and honey glaze:

$1/2$ cup honey

$1/4$ cup freshly squeezed orange juice

2 tablespoons freshly squeezed lime juice

2 tablespoons light brown sugar

1 teaspoon ground cinnamon

1. Preheat a grill to medium heat.

2. Rinse the halved Cornish hens under cold running water. Pat them dry. Rub the hens with the olive oil and sprinkle them with salt, pepper, and paprika. Place a lemon half and a rosemary sprig into each portion of Cornish hen.

3. Place the hens on the grill, cover, and grill for about 35 minutes, turning once. When the hens are fully cooked, remove them from the grill.

4. Meanwhile, make the citrus and honey glaze: In a medium saucepan over medium heat, whisk the honey, orange juice, lime juice, brown sugar, and ground cinnamon. Cook for 2 to 3 minutes, or until smooth and hot.

5. Drizzle the citrus and honey glaze over the grilled Cornish hens.

139

CARIBBEAN PAN-SEARED SNAPPER ESCOVITCH

Make this when you want to mentally escape to the Caribbean, and feel free to substitute any firm-fleshed white fish for the snapper.

SERVES 4 TO 6 | LEVEL: SLAM DUNK

6 tablespoons extra-virgin olive oil

1 small yellow onion, cut into julienne strips

1/2 red bell pepper, cut into julienne strips

1/2 green bell pepper, cut into julienne strips

1/2 yellow bell pepper, cut into julienne strips

2 carrots, cut into julienne strips

3 cloves garlic, minced

2 scallions, sliced (white and light green parts)

Kosher salt to taste

1 teaspoon cracked black pepper, plus more to taste

1 teaspoon sugar

3 tablespoons stemmed, chopped fresh cilantro

3 tablespoons white vinegar

Juice of 1/2 lime

Juice of 1/2 orange

1 1/2 pounds red snapper fillets

1 lemon, cut into wedges

1. In a large saute pan, heat 2 tablespoons of the olive oil over medium-high heat until very hot. Add the onion, red bell pepper, green bell pepper, yellow bell pepper, carrots, garlic, scallions, salt, and the teaspoon cracked black pepper. Sauté the vegetables for 3 minutes or until they soften and wilt.

2. Stir in the sugar, cilantro, vinegar, lime juice, and orange juice. Bring the sauce to a simmer over medium heat, reduce the heat to low, and cook, stirring, for 2 minutes or until it is hot and bubbly.

140

3. Season the red snapper fillets with salt and pepper to taste. In another sauté pan, heat the remaining 4 tablespoons olive oil over high heat until it smokes. Sear the fillets, skin side down, for 3 minutes. Flip over the fillets and cook on the other side for about 3 minutes, or until the flesh is firm and flaky, and the skin bright orange.

4. Spoon some of the sauce over the fillets, and garnish with the lemon wedges.

PAN-ROASTED SALMON WITH FRESH TOMATO SALSA

This springtime favorite is light, refreshing, and easy on the cook since you just pour the marinade over the fish and let it sit while you assemble a salad or side dish. Don't let the salmon stay in the marinade longer than about 30 minutes, though, or it may turn mushy. Once you've taken it out of the hot pan and paired it with my Fresh Tomato Salsa, this is a great meal to enjoy in the garden with a nice glass of crisp Pinot.

SERVES 4 | LEVEL: JUMP SHOT

1 pound Atlantic salmon fillet

1/2 cup extra-virgin olive oil

1/4 cup stemmed, chopped fresh cilantro leaves

2 tablespoons freshly squeezed lime juice

1/2 tablespoon Cajun spice

Kosher salt and freshly ground pepper to taste

1/2 cup white wine

Fresh Tomato Salsa (page 36)

1. Cut the salmon into 4 portions. In a small bowl, whisk 1/4 cup of the olive oil, the cilantro, lime juice, Cajun spice, salt, and pepper. Arrange the salmon in a shallow pan. Pour the marinade over the salmon. Allow to marinate for about 10 minutes.

2. Place a heavy sauté pan over medium-high heat for 1 minute. Pour the remaining 1/4 cup of olive oil into the pan. Transfer the salmon to the pan and sear it for about 2 minutes on each side. Slowly pour in the white wine, and cook the salmon on medium heat for another 3 minutes or until it is pink and opaque.

3. When the salmon is cooked, transfer it from the sauté pan to a serving platter. Add additional salt and pepper, if desired. Serve the salmon with Fresh Tomato Salsa.

"This dish was tough for me at first. I didn't want to ever cook fish, but Chef got me right. Another swish off the court!"

143

ALMOND-CRUSTED SOLE WITH GINGER-LIME BEURRE BLANC

Beurre blanc (in French, this means "white butter") is a classic sauce that typically has butter, wine, shallots, and vinegar, but it's even better with fresh lime juice. This is a great dish to serve for company. If you like, substitute another firm white fish, such as cod or scrod.

SERVES 4 TO 6 | LEVEL: JUMP SHOT

For the ginger-lime beurre blanc:

2 tablespoons finely chopped shallot

1 tablespoon grated fresh ginger

3 tablespoons freshly squeezed lime juice

$1/4$ cup dry white wine

$1/2$ cup (1 stick) unsalted butter

Kosher salt and freshly ground black pepper to taste

For the almond-crusted sole:

$1/2$ cup panko bread crumbs

$1/2$ cup freshly grated Parmesan cheese

$1/3$ cup chopped almonds

2 tablespoons stemmed, chopped fresh parsley

1 teaspoon lemon zest

6 3-ounce sole fillets

Kosher salt and freshly ground black pepper to taste

3 teaspoons extra-virgin olive oil

1. Make the ginger-lime beurre blanc: In a medium saucepan, combine the shallot, ginger, lime juice, and wine. Bring to a simmer over medium heat. Reduce the heat to low and simmer until the liquid is reduced to about 2 tablespoons. Whisk in the butter, 2 tablespoons at a time, until it is melted. Season the beurre blanc with salt and pepper. Remove from the heat and set aside.

2. Make the almond-crusted sole: Preheat the oven to 350°F.

3. In a medium bowl, combine the panko, Parmesan cheese, almonds, parsley, and lemon zest. Sprinkle the sole fillets with salt and pepper. Arrange them in a single layer in a baking pan. Brush the tops of the fillets with the olive oil. Cover the tops of the fillets with the almond mixture. Bake the fillets for 6 to 8 minutes, or until they flake easily with a fork.

4. Serve the beurre blanc over the sole fillets.

HERB-CRUSTED SEA BASS WITH CHAMPAGNE CURRY CREAM

Sea bass is a great choice for this dish, since it is lean to moderately fatty, and thus takes well to sautéing as well as a variety of cooking methods. For this dish, it's dressed up with a great curry-flavored sauce. Be sure to use very fresh curry powder as it really brings out the flavor of the fish.

SERVES 6 | LEVEL: JUMP SHOT

For the herb-crusted sea bass:

$1/4$ cup stemmed, chopped fresh parsley

$1/4$ cup stemmed, chopped fresh dill

$1/4$ cup chopped fresh basil

2 cloves garlic, minced

6 sea bass fillets, deboned

Kosher salt and freshly ground black pepper to taste

$1/4$ cup extra-virgin olive oil

For the Champagne curry cream:

2 tablespoons unsalted butter

3 cloves garlic, minced

1 shallot, chopped

$1/2$ cup stemmed, chopped fresh cilantro

2 teaspoons curry powder

$1/2$ cup Champagne

$1/4$ cup heavy cream

Kosher salt and freshly ground black pepper to taste

1. Make the fish: On a large, shallow plate, combine the parsley, dill, basil, and garlic. Season the sea bass fillets with salt and pepper. Top each fillet with some of the herb mixture.

2. In a large sauté pan, heat the olive oil over medium heat until it shimmers. Add the fillets, making sure not to overcrowd them. Sauté the fillets on each side for 3 minutes, or until thoroughly cooked. The fish should flake easily when done.

147

3. Meanwhile, make the Champagne curry cream: In a medium saucepan, melt the butter over medium heat. Add the garlic, shallot, and cilantro. Sauté for 3 minutes. Reduce the heat and stir in the curry powder. Simmer for 1 minute. Carefully pour in the Champagne and cook, stirring, for 2 minutes. Add the heavy cream, salt, and pepper. Stir until well blended. Top the fish with the Champagne curry cream or serve it on the side.

PAN-SEARED BAY SCALLOPS WITH ARUGULA SALAD

Sweet, succulent bay scallops, which are much smaller than sea scallops, are seared quickly in butter and oil, then served over arugula and topped with a zesty lemon vinaigrette. You'll love this salad so much you may serve it on its own, with other types of seafood or poultry.

SERVES 4 | LEVEL: JUMP SHOT

For the arugula salad:

3 cups arugula, washed, dried, and trimmed

1 shallot, thinly sliced

1 large cucumber, diced

1 large tomato, diced

For the lemon vinaigrette:

3 tablespoons freshly squeezed lemon juice

$^{1}/_{2}$ cup extra-virgin olive oil

1 tablespoon minced shallot

$1^{1}/_{2}$ teaspoons Dijon mustard

$^{1}/_{2}$ teaspoon sugar

$^{1}/_{2}$ teaspoon freshly grated lemon zest

Sea salt and freshly ground black pepper to taste

For the scallops:

$1^{1}/_{4}$ pounds bay scallops

Sea salt and freshly ground black pepper to taste

2 teaspoons unsalted butter

2 teaspoons extra-virgin olive oil

1. Make the arugula salad: In a large bowl, toss the arugula, shallot, cucumber, and tomato.

2. Make the vinaigrette: In a small bowl, whisk the lemon juice, olive oil, shallot, Dijon mustard, sugar, lemon zest, salt, and pepper.

3. Make the scallops: Rinse the scallops in cold water and pay them dry. Season them on all sides with salt and pepper. Heat the butter and the oil in a large sauté pan over high heat just until they begin to smoke.

149

4. Add the scallops in a single layer, making sure they don't touch one another, and sear them for about 2 minutes per side. When they develop a golden crust and are thoroughly cooked, remove them from the pan.

5. To assemble the dish: Distribute the salad among 4 serving plates. Top each portion of salad with some of the cooked scallops. Drizzle the lemon vinaigrette over each serving, and sprinkle with additional salt and pepper, if desired.

PAELLA

Though traditional paella features several kinds of seafood, this is a little bit different, with lamb sausage and grouper replacing the lobster, squid, and octopus. When you want to impress your company, this is a great dish to choose. Make this in a paella pan, which has two handles and is about 14 inches across, or in a large, heavy skillet.

SERVES 4 TO 6 | LEVEL: SLAM DUNK

2 whole chickens, cut into serving pieces

Kosher salt and freshly ground black pepper to taste

$\frac{1}{2}$ tablespoon paprika

$\frac{1}{4}$ cup Chef Max's Spice Blend (page 41)

3 tablespoons extra-virgin olive oil

1 pound lamb sausage, cut up

6 garlic cloves, diced

1 large yellow onion, diced

$\frac{1}{2}$ red bell pepper, cored, seeded, and diced

$\frac{1}{2}$ green bell pepper, cored, seeded, and diced

3 cups arborio rice

1 tablespoon saffron

8 cups Chicken Stock (page 27)

1 pound grouper, cut into large dice

1 pound fresh string beans, trimmed

2 tomatoes, diced

2 cups fresh or frozen peas

$\frac{1}{2}$ cup stemmed, chopped fresh parsley

3 lemons, quartered

$\frac{1}{2}$ cup stemmed, chopped fresh cilantro

1. Place the chicken into a bowl and sprinkle it with the salt, pepper, paprika, and Chef Max's Spice Blend.

2. Heat the olive oil in a paella pan or a large skillet over medium-high heat for 1 minute. When it is very hot, add the lamb sausage and the chicken, sprinkle with a little additional salt and pepper, and cook, stirring, for 6 to 8 minutes or until the meats are nicely browned.

151

3. Stir in the garlic, onion, and red and green pepper, and cook for 2 to 3 minutes or until they are soft. Stir in the rice and saffron. Cook, stirring constantly, for about 3 minutes over medium heat.

4. Stir in $3^1/_2$ cups of the chicken stock and cook, stirring, for about 10 minutes. As the stock starts to evaporate, add more. Stir in the grouper, string beans, tomatoes, peas, and parsley. Cook over medium-high heat, keeping an eye on how much stock is in the pan. When the stock is absorbed by the rice, add a little bit more to the pan and continue to cook the paella. Continue to add stock, and to cook, stirring, until the rice is tender and still quite moist. The total cooking time will be 25 to 30 minutes. Serve the paella in large bowls, garnished with lemon wedges and cilantro.

SALMON PINWHEELS WITH GARLIC HERB CREAM CHEESE

Lots of fresh herbs, along with garlic, give the cream cheese in this dish a great flavor. You can make this ahead of time and keep it in the refrigerator until serving time.

SERVES 8 TO 10 | LEVEL: JUMP SHOT

8 ounces cream cheese, softened

2 tablespoons minced shallot

2 tablespoons minced garlic

1 teaspoon stemmed, chopped fresh dill

1 teaspoon stemmed, chopped fresh parsley

2 tablespoons chopped fresh chives

2 pounds smoked salmon fillets, skinless and boneless

Salt and freshly ground black pepper to taste

1 lemon, cut into wedges

1. In a small bowl, combine the cream cheese, shallot, garlic, dill, parsley, and chives.

2. Spread each piece of smoked salmon with a layer of the seasoned cream cheese. Starting at one end, roll each salmon strip up tightly so that it looks like a pinwheel. Secure each pinwheel with a wooden toothpick.

3. Place the pinwheels in a single layer on a large platter and freeze them for 30 minutes. Remove the toothpicks from the pinwheels. Squeeze some fresh lemon juice over the pinwheels and arrange them on a serving platter.

153

COCONUT AND CORN SALAD

This side dish is a traditional Caribbean salad, and it's good with chicken or fish. Broiling the corn for just a minute or so keeps it nice and crunchy. Don't use sweetened shredded coconut in this dish. Find coconut flakes in a gourmet shop or make your own by grating fresh coconut on a Microplane grater.

SERVES 4 | LEVEL: LAYUP

6 ears fresh corn

1 cup coconut flakes

¼ cup chopped red onion

2 tablespoons chopped fresh basil

½ cup mayonnaise

1 tablespoon freshly squeezed lemon juice

Kosher salt and freshly ground black pepper to taste

1. Preheat the oven broiler.

2. Shuck the corn, being sure to remove all the silk from each ear. Broil the corn for a couple of minutes, just until it is nicely browned, turning it occasionally with a pair of tongs so that it will cook evenly.

3. When the corn is cool enough to handle, cut the kernels from the cobs and place them into a medium bowl. Sprinkle with the coconut flakes, red onion, and basil. Toss to combine.

4. Stir in the mayonnaise and the lemon juice, and mix well. Taste and season with salt and pepper as needed. Cover and chill. Serve the salad chilled or at room temperature.

154

TOMATO AND RADISH SLAW

This colorful, healthy salad is a great way to showcase radishes, so make it when you can find really fresh ones. Look for radishes that feel firm when you squeeze them and, if the leaves are still attached, make sure they're crisp and green. Cut away the leaves once you get the radishes home, and refrigerate the radishes for up to five days. Soaking radishes in ice water for a couple of hours will make them extra crisp.

SERVES 6 TO 8 | LEVEL: JUMP SHOT

2 cups cherry tomatoes, sliced in half lengthwise

1 cup shredded radish

$^1/_2$ cucumber, peeled and chopped

2 tablespoons chopped red onion

$^1/_2$ cup shredded carrot

2 tablespoons stemmed, chopped fresh parsley

3 tablespoons extra-virgin olive oil

2 tablespoons apple cider vinegar

$^1/_2$ teaspoon sugar

$^1/_4$ teaspoon garlic powder

1 tablespoon white and black sesame seeds

Kosher salt and freshly grated black pepper to taste

1. In a medium bowl, toss the cherry tomatoes, radish, cucumber, onion, carrot, and parsley.

2. Add the olive oil, apple cider vinegar, sugar, garlic powder, sesame seeds, salt, and pepper. Toss to combine. Refrigerate the salad until serving time.

ICEBERG WEDGE WITH BUTTERMILK BLUE CHEESE DRESSING, CANDIED TEARDROP TOMATOES, SHAVED ONIONS, CHIVES, AND EGGS

If you can't find teardrop tomatoes for this salad, use cherry tomatoes instead. You can make the dressing ahead of time, but wait until serving time to toss it with the salad.

SERVES 6 | LEVEL: LAYUP

For the buttermilk blue cheese dressing:

1 cup mayonnaise

1 cup blue cheese

$^1/_2$ cup sour cream

$^1/_4$ cup buttermilk

1 teaspoon chopped fresh garlic

1 teaspoon chopped fresh chives

2 tablespoons freshly squeezed lemon juice

Kosher salt and freshly ground black pepper to taste

For the candied teardrop tomatoes:

3 cups red and yellow teardrop tomatoes and/or cherry tomatoes

$^1/_4$ cup unsalted butter, melted

$^1/_2$ cup light brown sugar

Sea salt to taste

For the salad:

1 large head iceberg lettuce, washed, dried, and cut into 6 wedges

$^1/_2$ cup shaved red onion

$^1/_4$ cup chopped fresh chives

3 hard-boiled eggs, chopped

1. Make the buttermilk blue cheese dressing: In a medium bowl, whisk the mayonnaise, blue cheese, sour cream, buttermilk, garlic, chives, lemon juice, and salt and pepper. Cover and refrigerate.

2. Make the candied teardrop tomatoes: Preheat the oven to 350°F. In a bowl, toss the tomatoes with the butter, brown sugar, and salt. Place them on a

parchment paper–lined baking sheet and bake for about 10 minutes, or until they are wilted and soft.

3. To assemble the salad: Arrange the lettuce wedges on 6 plates. Top each wedge with some tomato, shaved red onion, chopped fresh chives, and chopped hard-boiled egg. Spoon some of the dressing onto each wedge, and serve immediately.

CUCUMBER AND TOMATO SALAD

English cucumbers, which are sometimes called hothouse cucumbers, are seedless and much longer than regular cucumbers. Look for them in the produce department, shrink-wrapped in plastic. Serve this crunchy, colorful salad on a bed of mixed greens, or as a garnish for chicken or fish.

SERVES 4 TO 6 | LEVEL: LAYUP

1/4 cup extra-virgin olive oil

1/4 tablespoon Champagne vinegar

1 tablespoon packed light brown sugar

1 teaspoon Dijon mustard

2 garlic cloves, minced

Kosher salt and freshly ground black pepper to taste

2 large beefsteak tomatoes, cut into medium dice

1/2 red onion, diced

2 English cucumbers, cut into medium dice

2 fresh basil leaves, cut into chiffonade

1/4 cup crumbled feta cheese

1. In a blender, combine the olive oil, vinegar, brown sugar, Dijon mustard, and half the minced garlic. Blend for 30 seconds or until smooth. Taste and add salt and pepper as needed.

2. In a large mixing bowl, combine the tomato, red onion, cucumber, remaining garlic, and basil. Pour the dressing over the vegetables and toss well. Sprinkle the feta cheese evenly over the top of the salad.

160

GRILLED CABBAGE WITH BALSAMIC BUTTER

Be sure to pull off and discard any wilted leaves from the cabbage head before starting this recipe. But don't actually remove the cores from the wedges, since the core helps the cabbage leaves stay together.

SERVES 6 TO 8 | LEVEL: LAYUP

For the cabbage:

1 head green cabbage

½ cup extra-virgin olive oil

Freshly ground black pepper to taste

1 tablespoon onion salt

1 tablespoon garlic salt

For the balsamic butter:

2 tablespoons extra-virgin olive oil

1 tablespoon minced shallot

1 teaspoon minced garlic

2 tablespoons balsamic vinegar

1 teaspoon light brown sugar

½ cup (1 stick) unsalted butter, at room temperature

1. Preheat a grill to medium for about 10 minutes, or preheat a grill pan over medium heat for about 5 minutes.

2. Trim any wilted leaves from the cabbage. Cut the cabbage into medium-sized wedges. Insert a wooden skewer into each cabbage wedge. Sprinkle the wedges with olive oil, pepper, onion salt, and garlic salt.

3. Grill the cabbage wedges for about 15 minutes, or until they are tender, brown, and crisp.

4. While the cabbage is on the grill, make the balsamic butter: Measure the olive oil into a medium saucepan and turn the heat to medium. Add the shallot and the garlic, and sauté for 1 or 2 minutes, or until soft. Stir in the balsamic vinegar and brown sugar. Simmer, whisking constantly, for 3 to 4 minutes or until the mixture thickens. Whisk in the butter until it melts.

5. Arrange the grilled cabbage on a serving platter and drizzle with the balsamic butter.

161

STEWED OKRA

Another classic dish to make with okra, this one is delicious with a roasted or fried chicken.

SERVES 4 | LEVEL: JUMP SHOT

1 tablespoon extra-virgin olive oil

1 pound okra, sliced lengthwise

$1/4$ cup Chicken Stock (page 27)

1 cup diced tomato

$1/4$ cup chopped yellow onion

$1/4$ cup cored, seeded, and chopped tricolor bell pepper

1 tablespoon chopped garlic

$1/2$ cup tomato paste

2 bay leaves

$1/2$ teaspoon crushed red pepper

1 teaspoon unsalted butter

Kosher salt and freshly ground black pepper to taste

1. Coat the bottom of a medium saucepan with olive oil and set it over medium heat for about 1 minute.

2. Add the okra, chicken stock, tomato, onion, bell pepper, garlic, tomato paste, bay leaves, and crushed red pepper. Bring the mixture to a boil, reduce the heat to a simmer, and cook for about 20 minutes, or until the vegetables are tender. If the mixture seems a little dry, add a bit more chicken stock.

3. Remove the bay leaves, transfer the okra to a serving bowl, and add the butter. Season with salt and pepper.

ZUCCHINI AND SQUASH FRITTERS

Kids of all ages love eating this with fried fish or fried chicken, but it also makes a great side dish for everyone. If you don't have blackening seasoning, you can substitute 1/2 teaspoon paprika.

SERVES 4 TO 6 | LEVEL: SLAM DUNK

2 zucchini, diced

2 summer squash, diced

2 tablespoons stemmed, chopped fresh thyme

1 shallot, chopped

2 garlic cloves, minced

Kosher salt and freshly ground black pepper to taste

1 teaspoon blackening seasoning

2 tablespoons extra-virgin olive oil, plus more for frying the fritters

2 eggs, lightly beaten

3 cups all-purpose flour

3/4 cup buttermilk

1. In a large bowl, combine the zucchini, squash, thyme, shallot, garlic, salt, pepper, and blackening seasoning. Mix very well.

2. In a large sauté pan, heat the 2 tablespoons olive oil over medium heat. Sauté the vegetables for 3 minutes or until they are soft. Drain off any accumulated liquid, and set the vegetables aside.

3. In a medium bowl, combine the eggs, flour, and buttermilk. Beat well. Stir in the sautéed vegetables so that you have a smooth batter.

4. Heat olive oil in a large, heavy skillet to a depth of about 1 inch until very hot. Make fritters by dropping about 2 tablespoons of the batter per fritter into the hot oil. Fry the fritters for 2 minutes or until they are golden brown

163

on one side, adding additional olive oil as needed to the pan. Flip them over and cook on the other side until nicely browned.

5. Repeat with all the remaining batter. You'll probably need to fry the fritters in several batches. Each batch will take 5 minutes to cook.

6. Drain the fritters on a paper towel–lined plate. Serve them hot.

GARLIC SHOESTRING FRIES

Russet potatoes, which have a low moisture content and a high starch content, are ideal for making into French fries. You may also see them labeled baking potatoes or even Idaho potatoes. In this dish, avoid using round white potatoes and round red potatoes, which are waxier and not as suited for making into fries.

SERVES 6 | LEVEL: SLAM DUNK

5 medium russet potatoes

3 cups vegetable oil

2 garlic cloves, minced

1/4 cup stemmed, chopped fresh parsley

Kosher salt and freshly ground black pepper to taste

Truffle oil, for drizzling

1. Wash the potatoes but do not peel them. Cut them into 1/4-inch strips on a mandoline or with a knife.

2. Heat the vegetable oil in a deep fryer according to the manufacturer's directions. When very hot, transfer the potato strips to the fryer and fry for 5 to 7 minutes or until soft inside and crisp and golden outside.

3. Remove the fries from the fryer and place them on a large platter. Toss the fries with the garlic, parsley, salt, and pepper. Drizzle with truffle oil and serve immediately.

166

BEER-BATTERED ONION RINGS

When picking out the onions to make this dish, look for ones that are heavy for their size. Dry, papery skins are a good quality in an onion, but soft spots are not. Once you cut into an onion, wrap it tightly in plastic wrap and refrigerate it. Since onions lose moisture rapidly once cut, use the onion within several days. These onion rings go great with steak, burgers, and all kinds of sandwiches. If you make these often, invest in a small countertop fryer so the onion rings are perfect every time.

SERVES 4 | LEVEL: SLAM DUNK

1 1/2 cups all-purpose flour

1/2 teaspoon mild paprika

1 teaspoon garlic powder

1/2 teaspoon freshly ground black
  pepper

1 12-ounce can light beer

3 cups vegetable oil

2 large yellow onions

Kosher salt to taste

1. Make the beer batter: In a large bowl, whisk the flour with the paprika, garlic powder, and pepper. Whisk in the beer until it is well combined with the dry ingredients.

2. Pour the vegetable oil into a deep fryer and heat it to 300°F.

3. Remove the skin from the onions and trim away the tips. Slice the onions horizontally into rings. Working in batches, toss the onion rings in the beer batter, shaking off any excess. Immediately drop the onion rings into the hot oil, being careful not to overcrowd them.

4. Fry the onion rings for about 3 minutes, turning them over once to guarantee even browning. Using a slotted spoon, remove the onion rings from the fryer and transfer them to a plate lined with paper towels. Season the onion rings with salt. Repeat the process until all the onion rings are used up. Serve immediately.

PIZZA

Use premade crusts or fresh pizza dough from the supermarket. Dust your work surface with a little flour and roll out each ball of dough to a diameter of about 10 inches. Feel free to change up the vegetables here and add in some of your own favorites.

SERVES 4 TO 6 | LEVEL: LAYUP

2 10-inch unbaked pizza crusts

1 cup marinara sauce

$^1/_2$ cup freshly grated Parmesan cheese

$^1/_2$ cup diced yellow onion

2 tablespoons chopped fresh oregano

2 fresh basil leaves, cut into chiffonade

$^1/_2$ cup thinly sliced turkey pepperoni

8 ounces sliced fresh mozzarella cheese

1. Preheat the oven to 500°F.

2. Place a large pizza stone on the bottom rack of the oven for 10 minutes. Remove the pizza stone from the oven. Place the crusts on the pizza stone. Spread each crust with $^1/_2$ cup of the marinara sauce. Sprinkle each crust with $^1/_4$ cup of the Parmesan cheese, $^1/_4$ cup of the diced onion, 1 tablespoon of the oregano, half of the basil, and $^1/_4$ cup of the turkey pepperoni.

3. Top each pie with some of the sliced mozzarella cheese.

4. Bake the pizzas for about 15 minutes, or until the sauce is bubbling and the crust is crispy and golden.

171

AMAR'E

Alexis and I both really enjoy having family and friends over. It's a relaxing way to spend time together. Barbecue is one of my favorites when we entertain, because you can visit with your guests while at the grill and make everything from meat to vegetables in one place.

When the team comes over to eat, I serve a buffet of healthy options. Because everyone has different preferences, I like to have a little of everything for people to enjoy. We make sure to have water, fresh fruit juices, and cocktails on hand and ready to serve. Here are some of our favorite cocktails. Each makes 1 serving.

A lot of our cocktail recipes call for something called *simple syrup*, sometimes called *sugar syrup*. While the ratio of sugar to water can vary, the recipe for these cocktails calls for a 1 to 1 ratio. To make simple syrup, boil 1 cup of water with 1 cup of sugar in a small saucepan, stirring until the sugar is dissolved and the mixture is clear. Store the syrup in the refrigerator, covered, for up to 1 week.

THE HARDY

2 ounces cognac (Dusse)

1/2 ounce Aperol

3/4 ounce lemon juice

1/2 ounce orange juice

3/4 ounce sage simple syrup

Lemon slice, for garnish

1. In a cocktail shaker, combine the cognac, Aperol, lemon juice, orange juice, and sage simple syrup. Shake very well.

2. Place an ice cube into a rocks glass. Pour the drink into the glass. Garnish with the lemon slice.

ALEXANDER'S ROMANCE

5 slices cucumber

1 ounce freshly squeezed
  lemon juice

1 ounce simple syrup (page 172)

2 ounces gin

1. In a cocktail shaker, muddle 5 thin slices of cucumber by mashing and crushing them with the back of a spoon. Combine the muddled cucumber, lemon juice, simple syrup, and gin.

2. Shake and strain into a rocks glass. Garnish with an additional cucumber slice, if desired.

PEARSECCO

1 ounce peach puree, thawed
    if frozen

½ ounce elderflower liqueur

2 ounces Prosecco

Thin slice of fresh pear, for
    garnish

1. In a flute or martini glass, combine the peach puree and elderflower liqueur.

2. Slowly pour in the Prosecco until it nearly reaches the rim.

3. Stir gently. Garnish the glass with a pear slice.

ESPRESSO STOUT MARTINI

Simple syrup and light brown sugar to rim the glass

2 ounces vodka

2 ounces (single shot) brewed espresso

2 ounces stout beer (preferably Guinness)

1 ounce simple syrup (page 172)

3 espresso beans, for garnish

1. Coat the rim of a martini glass with simple syrup and then brown sugar.

2. In a shaker, combine the vodka, espresso, stout beer, and simple syrup.

3. Add a few ice cubes and shake well. Strain into the martini glass. Garnish with the espresso beans.

MISS PIMM'S
MUDDLE

5 slices cucumber

2 ounces Pimm's liqueur

1 ounce vodka

1¼ ounces lemon juice

1¼ ounces simple syrup (page 172)

3 ounces water

Thin slices of lemon and cucumber, for garnish

1. In a cocktail shaker, mash and crush the 5 cucumber slices with the back of a spoon. Combine the cucumber, Pimm's liqueur, vodka, lemon juice, simple syrup, and water. Shake well.

2. Strain into a tall glass and garnish with lemon and cucumber.

GAME DAY

....

....

"AMAR'E

How I eat on a game day these days sure is different from when I first played ball as a kid. Back then, I was extremely focused on basketball but I didn't connect my performance with my dietary habits. I'd snack on things like chips and ice cream. After all, I was a teenager. Who didn't eat like that?

One of the only good things I ate as a teenager was fresh fruit. My grandfather had peach and orange trees growing in his yard. After school, before practice started, I'd head over to his house and pick myself some fruit to eat.

Gradually, as I got better at basketball, my eating habits improved. Once I started to play professionally, I had more resources to help me. The team nutritionist showed me how to get the most out of the food I was eating. Eventually, I got to a point in my career where I was able to hire a professional chef. And when Chef Max started to cook for us, I finally had someone to keep me on track and help me learn to eat and to cook in a healthy way.

Before a game, I feel my best if I eat a dinner of pasta. While I have animal protein in my diet during the season, usually I don't eat meat before a game. I like to have pasta primavera, Caesar salad, unsweetened tea, and ZICO water. Robust in flavor and very filling, vegetarian chili is a favorite, too. I need larger portions

180

of protein and carbs on game days because I burn a lot more calories than on practice days.

After a game, I like to enjoy a grilled rib eye steak, loaded baked potato, sautéed broccolini, and lemonade. I might even have a glass of red wine with my steak.

Of course, I train year-round, and even if there isn't practice during the off season, I need to maintain a healthy diet. When there's no practice or game, I am more conscious about how much I eat and I eat a little less. I'm not burning off all those calories, so of course I can't eat as much. I think it's important to be aware of how much and what we are eating.

MAX

Cooking for Amar'e on a game day is when I need to really get focused on meeting his needs for sustenance and for energy, all while making sure the food tastes good. As one of the Knicks' top players, he's all over the court and he burns through so many calories that he literally needs to take in thousands on a game day.

Food is the fuel he needs to be at the top of his game. Every dish has to count. With a caloric need of about 6,000 calories a day, Amar'e must eat energizing, balanced meals.

Amar'e frequently eats only vegetarian during the season. He won't eat any meat for weeks at a time. Animal protein can weigh him down and make him feel heavy. And heavy is not the way you want to feel when you're about to play basketball.

During the basketball season, keeping pace with Amar'e's nutritional needs keeps me a busy man. I shop daily for the best fruits and vegetables. I prepare a lot of whole grains and dishes made with beans. Coming up with vegetarian fare that he likes was once a challenge, though now he loves foods like kale. Turnips and rutabagas are no longer vegetables that I need to hide in other foods, and he loves dishes such as Coconut Beans and Rice (page 190), and Vegetable Stir-Fry (page 199). Once Amar'e realized that he liked vegetables, and that he didn't have to eat red meat to be assured of having enough energy to burn up the court for an entire game, he got interested in learning how to cook vegetarian. And when Amar'e puts his mind to something, he gives it his all. I don't need to tell you how quickly he mastered these game day dishes and made them his own! He's chosen his favorites—the ones he really likes to cook and that his family loves to eat even when it's *not* game day—to put into this chapter. Readers will find that, just like Amar'e, they start feeling healthier when they start cooking healthier. This chapter will inspire you to do so.

HUDDLE UP

We like to invite the team over at least once
or twice a month, either for a pre-game
buffet if we are going to watch a big football
game together or for a post-game dinner
if our team won that night. When we win,
the guys are always in a good mood and
they come over for some bonding time.

At my place, we like sitting around and watching football, especially if there's a big championship game on TV. We'll have some cold beer on hand, of course, and maybe one great cocktail. But the main attraction is the selection of small bites—just enough to tease the appetite. The guys like to walk around and talk, nibbling when they feel like it, instead of sitting down at the table in front of a big meal.

The menu really centers on finger foods. We'll often make some sliders—beef or pulled chicken are popular. Along with these, we'll serve some guacamole and homemade salsa with chips. The guys love our Grilled Lamb Chops with Tzatziki (page 130), Prime Steak Quesadillas (page 271), Salmon Cakes with Garlic Aioli (page 95), and Grilled Honey Garlic Chicken Wings (page 273). These all are big favorites when we're hanging out. And sometimes we just can't help the urge to make the guys some of our Buttermilk Fried Chicken (page 244) and Sweet Potato Waffles (page 68).

Whatever we're serving, it's pretty laid back. We like to keep it simple and just enjoy the game, the food, and the company.

VEGETABLE CRUDITÉS WITH AVOCADO HUMMUS

If you like having a healthy snack all ready for when you are starving, prepare both the vegetables and the hummus early in the morning and chill well. Even though it contains avocado, the dip can be made ahead of time and stored, covered, in the refrigerator. Blanching the vegetables and then plunging them into ice water helps retain their color and crispness. You can use whatever vegetables you like—whatever you're in the mood for or have on hand.

SERVES 6 | LEVEL: LAYUP

For the avocado hummus:

1 ripe avocado, peeled, pitted, and cut into large chunks

2 tablespoons stemmed, chopped fresh cilantro

1 cup canned chickpeas, drained and rinsed

1 tablespoon tahini

2 tablespoons freshly squeezed lemon juice

$1/2$ cup olive oil

Kosher salt and white pepper to taste

For the vegetables:

1 bunch asparagus, trimmed

$1/2$ head broccoli, cut into florets

4 ounces baby carrots

2 celery stalks, cut into thin sticks

$1/4$ green bell pepper, cored, seeded, and cut into julienne strips

$1/4$ red bell pepper, cored, seeded, and cut into julienne strips

$1/4$ yellow bell pepper, cored, seeded, and cut into julienne strips

$1/2$ bunch scallions, white parts trimmed away

6 cherry tomatoes

185

1. Make the avocado hummus: In the work bowl of a food processor, combine the avocado, cilantro, chickpeas, tahini, lemon juice, olive oil, salt, and pepper. Puree for 30 seconds or until smooth. Transfer the hummus to a serving bowl, cover it with plastic wrap, and refrigerate.

2. Bring 4 cups of water to a boil in a large saucepan. Make an ice bath by combining 3 cups of cold water and 3 cups of ice cubes in a large bowl. These will be used to prepare the vegetables.

3. Blanch the asparagus for 30 seconds in the boiling water. Using a slotted spoon, remove the asparagus from the boiling water and immediately transfer it to the ice water. After 1 minute, using the slotted spoon, remove the asparagus from the ice water bath and drain it into a colander.

4. In the same saucepan of boiling water, blanch the broccoli for about 30 seconds. Using a slotted spoon, remove the broccoli from the boiling water and transfer it to the ice water bath. After 1 minute, using the slotted spoon, remove it from the ice water bath and drain it into the colander. Pat the asparagus and the broccoli dry with a paper towel.

5. Arrange the asparagus; broccoli; baby carrots; celery sticks; green, red, and yellow bell pepper strips; trimmed scallions; and cherry tomatoes on a large, decorative platter. Serve with the hummus.

CUCUMBER CHIPS WITH ROASTED GARLIC AND TOMATO HUMMUS

This is healthy, keeps well, and as a bonus, it can be made ahead of time. You can even keep it overnight in the refrigerator. Leave the cucumbers unpeeled, since they're more colorful.

SERVES 6 TO 8 | LEVEL: LAYUP

4 whole garlic cloves, peeled

12 cherry tomatoes

6 fresh basil leaves

2 sprigs fresh thyme

$1/2$ cup extra-virgin olive oil

1 cup canned chickpeas, drained and rinsed

Juice of $1/2$ lemon

2 tablespoons tahini

Kosher salt and freshly ground black pepper

3 English cucumbers

1. Preheat the oven to 400°F.

2. In a medium bowl, toss the garlic cloves, cherry tomatoes, basil, thyme, and $1/4$ cup of the olive oil. Transfer the vegetables to a nonstick baking pan. Roast them for about 10 minutes or until they are very soft. Remove the vegetables from the oven and cool slightly.

3. In a food processor, combine the tomato mixture, chickpeas, lemon juice, tahini, remaining $1/4$ cup olive oil, salt, and pepper. Puree the mixture until smooth. Transfer the hummus to a serving dish. Cover and refrigerate.

4. Using a sharp knife, trim the ends from each of the cucumbers. Slice each one into $1/2$-inch-thick rounds. Arrange the cucumber chips on a platter. Serve them with the hummus.

187

PASTA PRIMAVERA

The tomato chutney gives this dish a lot of flavor. Store leftover chutney in the refrigerator, use it within a week.

SERVES 4 TO 6 | LEVEL: JUMP SHOT

For the tomato chutney:

1 tablespoon extra-virgin olive oil

2 garlic cloves, minced

2 ripe beefsteak tomatoes, diced

3 fresh basil leaves

$1/4$ cup sugar

Kosher salt and freshly ground black pepper to taste

For the vegetables:

2 yellow summer squash, ends removed, cut on the bias into $1/2$-inch-thick slices

2 zucchini, ends removed, cut on the bias into $1/2$-inch-thick slices

1 bunch asparagus, tough ends removed, cut into 2-inch lengths

2 carrots, cut on the bias into $1/2$-inch rounds

$1/4$ cup extra-virgin olive oil

Kosher salt and freshly ground black pepper to taste

1 tablespoon herbes de provence

$1/2$ cup white wine

1 teaspoon unsalted butter

1 pound bowtie pasta

Freshly grated Parmesan cheese, for topping

1. Make the tomato chutney: In a medium sauté pan, heat the olive oil over medium heat for 1 minute. Add the garlic and tomato and sauté for 1 minute. Add the basil, sugar, salt, and pepper. Sauté over medium-high heat for 10 minutes or until the mixture is reduced by half and the tomatoes look almost caramelized.

2. In a large bowl, combine the summer squash, zucchini, asparagus, carrots, olive oil, salt, pepper, and herbes de provence. Toss to coat the vegetables with the oil.

3. Preheat a large sauté pan over medium heat for 1 minute. Add the vegetables, and sauté for about 3 minutes. Add the wine and the butter. Turn off the heat.

4. Meanwhile, cook the bowtie pasta in a large pot of boiling, lightly salted water until al dente, following the directions on the box. Drain the pasta.

5. In a large bowl, toss the cooked pasta with the vegetables until well combined. Add $\frac{1}{2}$ cup of the tomato chutney and mix well. Season the pasta with salt and pepper, and sprinkle with some Parmesan cheese. Serve immediately.

" Before Chef Max, I ate out a lot, and this was a dish I would order most often. Chef makes an amazing Pasta Primavera, which the kids love! I try to copy the recipe on Chef's days off."

189

COCONUT BEANS AND RICE

This is definitely a main dish, but you could also think of it as a side dish when you are serving jerk chicken or roasted chicken for dinner. Scotch bonnet peppers are hot! Use just a quarter of one. It will flavor the dish much the same way that a bay leaf does, but it should be removed before you serve this so that no one will bite into it unknowingly. If you want, you may substitute one quarter of a habanero pepper for the Scotch bonnet pepper.

SERVES 4 TO 6 | LEVEL: JUMP SHOT

$1/4$ cup unsweetened flaked coconut

$1/4$ cup extra-virgin olive oil

$1/2$ yellow onion, diced

2 tablespoons tomato paste

2 garlic cloves, minced

2 cups uncooked jasmine rice

1 teaspoon grated fresh ginger

Kosher salt to taste

2 cups Chicken Stock (page 27)

2 cups coconut milk

1 cup canned kidney beans

1 tablespoon chopped fresh thyme

$1/4$ Scotch bonnet pepper

1. Preheat the oven to 350° F.

2. Spread out the coconut on a nonstick baking sheet, and toast it for 10 minutes or until golden brown. Set aside.

3. In a large saucepan or Dutch oven over medium-high heat, heat the olive oil for 1 minute. Add the onion and the tomato paste, and sauté for about 5 minutes or until the onion is beginning to brown.

4. Stir in the garlic and rice, and continue to sauté for another 2 or 3 minutes. Stir in the ginger, salt, chicken stock, coconut milk, and kidney beans. Sprinkle with the thyme. Add the $1/4$ Scotch bonnet pepper.

190

5. Bring the mixture to a boil over medium heat, reduce the heat to low, and cover the saucepan. Simmer the mixture for about 15 minutes.

6. Remove the cover from the saucepan and check the rice for doneness. If it's not quite done, continue to cook it for another 5 minutes or until tender. Remove from the heat and remove the Scotch bonnet pepper. Spoon into a serving dish, fluff with a fork, and sprinkle with the toasted coconut.

" When Chef came to L.A. the summer I got traded, he made oxtails, Coconut Beans and Rice, and cabbage. The Coconut Beans and Rice really stuck out. It's a good Caribbean dish with great flavor and the coconut milk makes it a standout. My team said, 'Amar'e, you have to hire this guy!' "

ROASTED ROOT VEGETABLES

Season these up and roast them off the night before you plan to serve them, then keep them in the refrigerator. You'll warm them up in a medium oven just before dinner. Though they're so good for snacking that you may not even think of them for a meal, these roasted root vegetables also are very good with fish, steak, or any kind of roasted meat. Be sure to not cut up the vegetables too small. Peel the carrots but consider leaving on the skins of most other vegetables. Leaving the skin on holds the integrity of the vegetable, and a lot of the nutrients are in the skin.

SERVES 6 TO 8 | LEVEL: JUMP SHOT

3 turnips, scrubbed and diced

3 carrots, peeled and diced

3 sweet potatoes, scrubbed and diced

3 beets, scrubbed and diced

3 parsnips, scrubbed and diced

3 rutabagas, scrubbed and diced

2 leeks, cleaned, trimmed, and roughly chopped

Kosher salt and freshly ground black pepper to taste

$1/2$ cup extra-virgin olive oil

$1/4$ cup balsamic vinegar

1 tablespoon chopped fresh thyme

3 garlic cloves, minced

1. Preheat the oven to 400°F.

2. Arrange the vegetables in a single layer on 2 large nonstick baking sheets. Sprinkle the vegetables with salt and pepper. Drizzle them with the olive oil and the balsamic vinegar. Sprinkle the vegetables with the thyme and the garlic.

3. Place the vegetables into the oven, and roast them for about 45 minutes, or until they are softened and beginning to turn golden brown. Transfer the vegetables to a large serving platter.

193

THREE-BEAN SALAD

This is a pregame deal because it's great as a snack. It's also a very flexible dish because you can add as many beans as you want, or use whatever kind is your own favorite. Chilling this salad for awhile allows the beans to soak up the dressing so it's an ideal dish to make the day before you serve it.

SERVES 4 TO 6 | LEVEL: LAYUP

1 cup canned white beans, drained and rinsed

1 cup canned kidney beans, drained and rinsed

1 cup canned black beans, drained and rinsed

$1/2$ bunch cilantro, stemmed and chopped

$1/4$ cup chopped tomato

$1/4$ cup chopped red onion

$1/4$ cup extra-virgin olive oil

$1/4$ cup Champagne vinegar

$1/4$ teaspoon ground cumin

1 tablespoon freshly squeezed lemon juice

2 tablespoons agave nectar

Kosher salt and freshly ground black pepper to taste

1. In a large bowl, combine the white beans, kidney beans, black beans, cilantro, tomato, and red onion.

2. In a small bowl, whisk the olive oil, vinegar, cumin, lemon juice, agave nectar, salt, and pepper.

3. Pour the dressing over the beans, and toss to coat. Chill the salad for several hours before serving.

COUSCOUS SALAD

This is another great travel snack, but you don't have to be traveling in order to enjoy it. If you don't plan to eat it right away, pack the dressing on the side, to add at the last minute.

SERVES 4 TO 6 | LEVEL: JUMP SHOT

$^1/_2$ butternut squash, diced

For the vinaigrette:

$^1/_4$ cup extra-virgin olive oil

$^1/_4$ cup freshly squeezed lemon juice

2 garlic cloves, finely minced

2 tablespoons stemmed, chopped cilantro

Kosher salt and freshly ground black pepper to taste

For the couscous:

2 cups Chicken Stock (page 27)

1 teaspoon extra-virgin olive oil

1 cup couscous

1 cucumber, peeled and diced

$^1/_2$ cup finely diced red onion

$^1/_2$ cup crumbled feta cheese

1 avocado, peeled, cored, and diced

1 green bell pepper, cored, seeded, and diced

Salt and freshly ground black pepper to taste

1. Preheat the oven to 400°F.

2. Arrange the squash on a nonstick baking sheet. Roast it for 20 minutes or until soft.

3. Make the vinaigrette: In a blender, combine the olive oil, lemon juice, garlic, and cilantro. Blend well. Sprinkle with salt and pepper to taste. Set aside.

4. Make the couscous: In a medium saucepan, bring the chicken stock to a boil. Stir in the olive oil and the couscous, cover, and remove from the heat. Allow the couscous to stand for 2 minutes. Uncover the couscous and fluff

195

it with a fork. If it's not quite done, add about $^1/_2$ cup extra broth, cover, and cook on low for 5 to 10 minutes or until fluffy.

5. In a large serving bowl, combine the couscous, cucumber, red onion, feta cheese, avocado, green bell pepper, and butternut squash. Add the vinaigrette and toss to combine. Taste, and add additional salt and pepper as needed.

VEGETABLE FRIED RICE

This pregame lunch is loaded with nutrients. If you want the fried rice to get nicely crisp, resist the urge to stir or toss it once you add the rice to the wok. Cooking the diced carrot and snow peas ahead of time means they'll be about as soft as the rest of the vegetables. Maggi seasoning is available in the international section of most supermarkets.

SERVES 6 | LEVEL: LAYUP

1/2 cup diced carrot

1/2 cup snow peas

1/2 cup sesame oil

1 yellow onion, chopped

3 garlic cloves, minced

2 tablespoons peeled, diced fresh ginger

1 red bell pepper, cored, seeded, and diced

1 green bell pepper, cored, seeded, and diced

1 yellow bell pepper, cored, seeded, and diced

3 celery stalks, chopped

1/4 cup cashews

3 scallions, sliced on the diagonal, white part separated from the green part

3 eggs, lightly beaten

Kosher salt and freshly ground black pepper to taste

4 cups cooked jasmine rice, cold

3 tablespoons Maggi seasoning

1 fresh pineapple, cored, peeled, and chopped

1. In a medium saucepan, bring 3 cups of water to a boil. Add the diced carrot and snow peas and cook for 2 or 3 minutes. Drain the vegetables and set them aside.

2. Heat a large wok over medium-high heat for 1 minute. Pour in 1/4 cup of the sesame oil. When it shimmers, add the onion, garlic, ginger, bell peppers, celery, cashews, carrot, snow peas, and white part of the scallions to the wok. Stir-fry for about 2 minutes. Transfer all the vegetables to a large bowl.

197

3. Pour 2 more tablespoons of the sesame oil into the wok. Add the eggs, season with salt and pepper, and stir-fry until the eggs are cooked, about 30 seconds, but still light and fluffy. Transfer the eggs to a medium bowl and set aside.

4. Pour the remaining 2 tablespoons of the sesame oil into the wok. Add the rice and stir-fry it for 2 minutes, using a large wooden spoon to break up any clumps. Continue to cook the rice for another 2 minutes, without stirring it. Add the scallion greens and toss until they are well combined with the rice.

5. Transfer the rice to a large serving bowl. Add the vegetable mixture and the egg mixture. Toss to combine. Sprinkle with the Maggi seasoning, toss well, and top with as much of the chopped pineapple as you like.

"Because my wife and kids love Chinese food, we often order in on Saturdays and we always order stir-fry. But now I whip it up myself often. The kids get in the kitchen with me on this recipe; they love playing with the wok."

VEGETABLE STIR-FRY

When making this hearty stir-fry, choose small heads of bok choy. Always buy bok choy with firm, white stalks and crisp, bright-green leaves.

SERVES 4 TO 6 | LEVEL: JUMP SHOT

1 pound lo mein noodles

1/4 cup sesame oil

1 white onion, chopped

1 bell pepper (use red, yellow or green), cored, seeded, and cut in julienne strips

1/4 pound shiitake mushrooms, sliced

3 celery stalks, sliced on the bias

2 carrots, sliced on the bias

1 teaspoon grated fresh ginger

3 garlic cloves, sliced thin

4 heads bok choy, trimmed and quartered

2 tablespoons oyster sauce

1/4 cup Maggi seasoning

1/4 cup pineapple juice

2 tablespoons sesame seeds

3 scallions, sliced on the bias

1. In a large pot of boiling water, cook the lo mein noodles according to package directions. Drain and set aside.

2. Meanwhile, preheat a large wok over medium-high heat for 1 minute. Pour in the sesame oil and heat it until it shimmers. Add the white onion, bell pepper, mushrooms, celery, carrots, ginger, and garlic. Stir-fry for 2 minutes. Add the bok choy and cook for 1 minute. Stir in the oyster sauce, Maggi seasoning, and pineapple juice. Remove from the heat.

3. Sprinkle the stir-fry with the sesame seeds. Serve in large bowls, garnished with the scallions.

199

VEGETARIAN CHILI

You might think that a quarter cup of chili powder sounds like a lot, but this chili, while spicy, isn't overly hot. For this dish, use the tricolor peppers, which come three in a package and have one each of the red, green, and yellow peppers.

SERVES 4 TO 6 | LEVEL: JUMP SHOT

3 tablespoons extra-virgin olive oil

1 cup chopped yellow onion

$1/4$ cup chopped celery

1 cup chopped tricolor bell pepper (red, green, and yellow)

4 garlic cloves, chopped

$1/4$ pound shiitake mushrooms, trimmed and sliced

$1/4$ cup tomato paste

3 tablespoons ground cumin

1 chipotle chile pepper in adobo, diced

$1/4$ cup chili powder

2 tablespoons garlic powder

2 tablespoons onion powder

1 bunch cilantro leaves, stemmed and chopped

1 pound ground tofu

2 cups Vegetable Stock (page 24)

Grated Mexican blend cheese and sour cream, for garnish

1. Preheat a 10-quart stockpot over medium heat for 1 minute. Add the olive oil, onion, celery, bell pepper, garlic, shiitake mushrooms, and tomato paste. Sauté for about 10 minutes, stirring constantly. Reduce the heat to a simmer.

2. Add the cumin, chipotle, chili powder, garlic powder, onion powder, 3 tablespoons of the chopped cilantro, tofu, and vegetable stock. Simmer, stirring occasionally, for about 45 minutes. Serve in bowls, garnishing each serving with some grated Mexican blend cheese, a dollop of sour cream, and a little chopped cilantro.

201

VEGETABLE SOUP

Serve this soup as a lunch dish along with a sandwich. Thick, hearty, and filling, it's great to make ahead and then reheat.

SERVES 4 TO 8 | LEVEL: JUMP SHOT

¹/₄ cup extra-virgin olive oil

2 celery stalks, roughly chopped

2 carrots, roughly chopped

1 leek, cleaned thoroughly, roughly chopped

2 turnips, trimmed and roughly chopped

1 potato, peeled and cut into 1-inch cubes

1 tablespoon chopped fresh ginger

5 garlic cloves, chopped

Kosher and freshly ground black pepper to taste

2 large tomatoes, cored and chopped

1 16-ounce can red kidney beans

3 bay leaves

1 bunch cilantro, stemmed

1 teaspoon red pepper flakes or to taste, for sprinkling

1. Preheat a large stockpot over medium heat for 1 minute. Add the olive oil, then the celery, carrots, leek, turnips, potato, ginger, and garlic. Season with some salt and pepper.

2. Sauté the vegetables for about 5 minutes or until soft and translucent. Add 4 quarts of water, the chopped tomato, red beans, bay leaves, and half the cilantro. Reduce the heat to a simmer and simmer the soup for about 45 minutes, stirring occasionally, until all the vegetables are very tender.

3. Remove the bay leaves from the soup. Season the soup to taste with salt and pepper. Serve it in large bowls, garnished with the remaining cilantro and sprinkled with the red pepper flakes.

202

"This is a good soup for wintry days, and I like to add ginger in there to keep me nice and healthy."

203

COCONUT CURRY CARROT SOUP

This soup is delicious hot or, in hot weather, you can eat it chilled. It's a great way to get in some extra vegetables. If you don't have an immersion blender, puree the soup in batches in a regular blender.

SERVES 6 | LEVEL: JUMP SHOT

4 cups Vegetable Stock (page 24)

8 carrots, chopped

1 onion, diced

2 tablespoons chopped fresh ginger

3 tablespoons chopped fresh thyme

2 bay leaves

3 garlic cloves, minced

2 potatoes, peeled and diced

1 cup coconut milk

Kosher salt and freshly ground black pepper to taste

$1/2$ cup sour cream

Juice of $1/2$ lemon

1 tablespoon stemmed, chopped fresh cilantro

Dash of white pepper

1. In a large saucepan, bring the vegetable stock to a boil.

2. Add the carrots, onion, ginger, thyme, bay leaves, garlic, and potatoes. Simmer for about 1 hour, stirring occasionally, until all the vegetables are very soft.

3. Remove the bay leaves. Then, using an immersion blender, puree the soup until smooth.

4. Stir in the coconut milk, and season with salt and pepper. Strain the soup through a fine-mesh sieve china cap.

5. In a small bowl, whisk the sour cream with the lemon juice, cilantro, and white pepper. When well mixed, transfer to a bottle with a squeeze top. Chill for at least an hour.

6. About 15 minutes before you plan to serve the soup, remove the bottle of sour cream from the refrigerator. Ladle the soup into large soup bowls. Garnish each serving by squeezing some of the sour cream in a zigzag pattern onto the soup.

SWEET VICTORY

....

PEANUT BUTTER COOKIE SANDWICHES 211

PEACH COBBLER 214

WHITE CHOCOLATE AND BANANA BREAD PUDDING 216

CHOCOLATE MOUSSE 219

THREE-LAYER CARROT CAKE 220

RUM PECAN CHOCOLATE BROWNIES 223

VANILLA BEAN ICE CREAM 224

SWEET POTATO PIE 225

LEMON BARS 228

RED VELVET SWIRL CHEESECAKE 229

....

"AMAR'E

I try to avoid desserts, especially when I am in season, because it's important that I concentrate on eating a well-balanced diet and if I do that, there's no room for sweets. Once in a great while, though, I give in and have a chocolate chip cookie or a scoop of ice cream.

On the occasions that I treat myself, ice cream is my first choice. My favorite flavor is butter pecan. But when Max and I make homemade Vanilla Bean Ice Cream (page 224), I must admit this is a close second.

Although I don't eat dessert very often, our kids are allowed to have dessert when they finish a sensible dinner. We have rules, though. In addition to being responsible for eating all of their dinner, the kids have to take care of their own dishes before they are allowed dessert. Like me, the kids are all ice cream lovers, and there is always ice cream in the freezer.

Besides ice cream, we love the cookies, cakes, and pies that Max makes for us, and has taught me to make. We like to spend time mixing up Rice Krispies Treats or brownies together. It's kind of our thing as a family. The kids' favorite thing to make is dessert. Sometimes we save the homemade brownies or cookies for dessert that night, but most of the time, we just can't keep from eating them as soon as they come out of the oven.

Some of my favorite desserts are from my childhood, like Peach Cobbler (page 214) and red velvet cake. I always choose red velvet for my birthday cake, and Alexis and I had a red velvet cake for a very important occasion: our wedding. Since our children have adopted it as their favorite cake, too, we have red velvet cake for every birthday. Max has started making Red Velvet Swirl Cheesecake (page 229) so that the portion size is just right for the kids. Because when it comes to dessert, it's really all about the kids anyway.

MAX

My desserts often have a Southern accent, though my Bahamian roots also play a big part in the variety of sweets I create.

I love going back to see family in Detroit and Florida, and food (dessert included) is always the center point of a trip to see my relatives. Of course, we make some of the traditional desserts from my childhood when I visit. Thanksgiving and Christmas are always an amazing time, when we bake Sweet Potato Pie (page 225), sweet potato cheesecake, and, of course, red velvet cake. (That's a favorite in my family, too.)

Amar'e and I occasionally whip up a dessert together. While he is careful not to let the kids eat too many sweets, he's down with a big, festive cake or creamy rich pudding after a meal for guests. His kids love dessert so I created some just for them, like my Peanut Butter Cookie Sandwiches (page 211). The peanut butter filling is easy to make, and the whole family likes to assemble sandwiches with the cookies and the filling.

209

Dessert's not something that we have every day, but when we do, it's always something really special. And we always prep a variety, so everyone can have a taste of various desserts. Because dessert is for meant for sharing with the people you love.

WINNING WAYS TO DECORATE TREATS

When they're in the mood to cook, the kids love making and decorating sweets more than anything else. Brownies are a big favorite at our house, as are Rice Krispies Treats, which they make sometimes with Fruity Pebbles. Decorating cookies and cupcakes can keep them busy for a very long time, and it's a great family project.

When the kids want to take over the kitchen and display their artistic side with frosting and sprinkles, here's how to score big

•To cut down on mess, cover your kitchen table with white butcher paper. You can simply wrap it up and discard it later.

•If you're decorating with a group of kids, have both the cookies or cupcakes and the icing made ahead of time. Give each child his or her own work station at the table with some cookies and bowls of decorating supplies.

•Have plenty of decorations arranged in shallow bowls and put a little spoon into each bowl. Suggested decorations: mini marshmallows, colorful sanding sugar, peanuts, raisins, chocolate sprinkles, rainbow sprinkles, M&M's or mini M&M's, and red hots. If you have little tubes of icing on hand, the kids can glue decorations like raisins or M&M's onto unfrosted cookies.

•Demonstrate to the kids how to spread icing on a cupcake or a cookie. Then give them each a little plastic knife and let them try it on their own.

•Sit back, relax, and let your child's imagination take over.

210

PEANUT BUTTER COOKIE SANDWICHES

If you don't have a nonstick baking sheet, line a regular baking sheet with parchment paper. And feel free to make the dough ahead of time. Just be sure to remove it from the refrigerator about 30 minutes before you plan to make the cookies.

MAKES 1½ DOZEN | LEVEL: LAYUP

For the cookies:

1 cup (2 sticks) unsalted butter, at room temperature

1 cup granulated sugar

1 cup packed dark brown sugar

2 large eggs

½ cup chopped Reese's Peanut Butter Cups

1 cup peanut butter

1 teaspoon vanilla extract

3 cups all-purpose flour

2 teaspoons baking soda

¼ teaspoon kosher salt

For the filling:

½ cup peanut butter

3 cups confectioners' sugar

4 tablespoons whole milk

2 tablespoons honey

1 teaspoon vanilla extract

1. Preheat the oven to 350°F.

2. In a large mixing bowl, with an electric mixer set on medium speed, beat the butter, granulated sugar, and brown sugar until creamy. Beat in the eggs, one at a time, then mix in the chopped Reese's Peanut Butter Cups, peanut butter, and vanilla.

3. Add the flour, baking soda, and salt. Stir by hand until well blended.

4. With your hands, roll the dough into 1-inch balls. Arrange the cookies on a large nonstick baking sheet, leaving about 1½ inches of space between them. Bake the cookies for 8 to 10 minutes, or until they are set and golden brown. Remove the cookies from the oven and, using a spatula, transfer them to a wire rack to cool. Repeat with the remaining dough.

211

5. Make the filling: In a large mixing bowl, with an electric mixer set on medium speed, beat the peanut butter, confectioners' sugar, milk, honey, and vanilla extract until smooth and creamy.

6. To assemble the cookie sandwiches, turn one cookie flat side up and spread with about $1^1/_2$ teaspoons of filling. Top with another cookie, with the flat side facing the filling. Continue to make cookie sandwiches until all the cookies have been used.

213

PEACH COBBLER

This dessert is actually better when it's made with frozen peaches, which have less water than fresh, and which really take on the flavor of the other ingredients.

SERVES 6 | LEVEL: JUMP SHOT

1 sheet puff pastry, thawed according to package directions

3 cups frozen sliced peaches

¼ cup sugar

1 tablespoon vanilla extract

1 teaspoon ground cinnamon

1 teaspoon ground nutmeg

1 tablespoon unsalted butter, softened

1. Preheat the oven to 350°F.

2. Using a sharp knife, trim the puff pastry so that it fits onto a 1-quart baking dish.

3. In a medium bowl, toss the peaches with the sugar, vanilla, ground cinnamon, ground nutmeg, and butter. Transfer the peach mixture to the baking dish.

4. Place the puff pastry on top of the peaches and press down gently. Cut an *X* in the top of the puff pastry.

5. Bake the cobbler for 40 to 50 minutes, or until the filling is bubbling and the crust is golden brown. Serve the cobbler warm, with ice cream if desired.

214

"This is one of my favorite desserts. My aunt Dilly comes to visit a few times each year and every time she does, she has to get in the kitchen and make my favorite. It's rich and sweet, with a lot of love. I like to add some vanilla ice cream on top."

215

WHITE CHOCOLATE AND BANANA BREAD PUDDING

This is best served warm, though you can make it a few hours ahead of time. Chop up bars of white chocolate, or simply make your life easy and buy a bag of white chocolate chunks. If you like, top the pudding with ice cream and drizzle with caramel sauce.

SERVES 8 | LEVEL: JUMP SHOT

Unsalted butter for the baking dish

1 loaf challah bread, cut into 1-inch cubes

2 cups white chocolate chunks

3 large bananas, sliced

$^{1}/_{2}$ cup (1 stick) unsalted butter, melted and cooled

2 cups whole milk

2 cups heavy cream

$^{2}/_{3}$ cup sugar

2 tablespoons vanilla extract

8 large eggs

1. Preheat the oven to 350°F.

2. Lightly butter a deep-sided 10-inch square baking dish.

3. Arrange the challah bread cubes in the baking dish. Top with the white chocolate chunks and the banana slices. Drizzle with the melted butter.

4. In a large saucepan, combine the milk, heavy cream, sugar, and vanilla. Bring to a boil, reduce the heat, and simmer, stirring constantly, until the sugar dissolves. Remove the saucepan from the heat. Cool slightly.

5. In a large mixing bowl, whisk the eggs until they are foamy. Slowly pour the milk-cream mixture into the eggs, stirring constantly until well mixed. Pour the mixture over the bread cube mixture, and allow it to stand for about 10 minutes so that the liquid will be absorbed by the bread.

6. Bake the pudding for about 1 hour, or until it is golden brown and set.

216

CHOCOLATE MOUSSE

You can make this ahead of time but keep in mind that the earlier you make it, the more it sets. If you like, skip the raspberries and mint leaves and garnish this with freshly grated orange zest or toasted coconut flakes.

SERVES 4 TO 6 | LEVEL: JUMP SHOT

4 egg yolks

4 tablespoons sugar

2 cups heavy cream

1$\frac{1}{2}$ cups chopped bittersweet chocolate, melted and cooled

1 tablespoon vanilla extract

Fresh raspberries and mint leaves, for garnish

1. In a medium saucepan, whisk the egg yolks, 2 tablespoons of the sugar, and $\frac{3}{4}$ cup of the cream. When the mixture is smooth, place the saucepan over medium heat and cook the mixture, stirring constantly, until it thickens. Do not allow the mixture to boil.

2. Remove the saucepan from the heat. Whisk in the chocolate and the vanilla extract. Transfer it to a large serving bowl, cover with plastic wrap, and refrigerate for about 1 hour.

3. In a medium mixing bowl, using a hand-held electric mixer set on medium speed, beat the remaining 1$\frac{1}{4}$ cup heavy cream with the remaining 2 tablespoons sugar until soft peaks form. Fold the whipped cream into the chocolate mixture. Cover and chill.

4. When ready to serve, spoon the mousse into serving bowls and garnish each bowl with raspberries and mint leaves.

219

THREE-LAYER CARROT CAKE

Everyone seems to have a recipe for carrot cake. This is a real classic, with a creamy, rich frosting spread between the layers and on the top and sides of the cake.

SERVES 6 TO 10 | LEVEL: SLAM DUNK

For the cake:

Unsalted butter, for greasing the pans

2 cups granulated sugar

1 1/2 cups vegetable oil

4 large eggs, at room temperature

2 cups all-purpose flour

1 teaspoon ground cinnamon

1 teaspoon ground nutmeg

2 teaspoons baking powder

2 teaspoons baking soda

1 teaspoon kosher salt

3 cups shredded carrot

1/2 cup chopped pecans

1/2 cup raisins

For the buttercream frosting:

1/2 cup (1 stick) unsalted butter, softened

8 ounces cream cheese, softened

3 cups confectioners' sugar

For garnish:

White chocolate shavings

1. Preheat the oven to 350°F.

2. Lightly butter three round 9-inch cake pans.

3. In a large mixing bowl, with an electric mixer, beat the sugar with the oil on medium speed for 1 minute or until well blended. Add the eggs, one at a time, beating well after each addition. Beat in the flour, cinnamon, nutmeg, baking powder, baking soda, and salt. Stir in the carrots, pecans, and raisins. Spoon the batter into the prepared pans. Bake for 30 to 35 minutes, or until a toothpick inserted into the center of the cake comes out clean.

220

4. Let the layers cool in the pans for 10 minutes. Remove the layers from the pans and cool them on a wire rack for 20 to 25 minutes.

5. Make the buttercream frosting: In the work bowl of an electric mixer, combine the butter, cream cheese, and confectioners' sugar. Beat on medium speed until light and creamy.

6. To assemble: Place one cake layer on a platter and spread the top with a layer of frosting. Top with another cake layer, and spread with another layer of frosting. Place the remaining cake layer on top, and frost the top and sides. Sprinkle the white chocolate shavings over the top of the cake.

To make the white chocolate shavings, slightly soften a four-inch bar of white chocolate in the microwave. Scrape the blade of a vegetable peeler lengthwise across the chocolate bar, creating curls. Refrigerate the curls for about 30 minutes to firm them up.

221

RUM PECAN CHOCOLATE BROWNIES

A delicious and sophisticated brownie, this one gets a little kick from the rum. You can buy chocolate milk premade at the store, or simply make it yourself with chocolate syrup. As these are very rich, cut them into small squares.

MAKES 24 BROWNIES | LEVEL: JUMP SHOT

$^1/_2$ pound (2 sticks) unsalted butter, plus additional for greasing the pan

1 cup semisweet or dark chocolate pieces

$^1/_4$ cup chocolate milk

$^2/_3$ cup all-purpose flour

$^1/_4$ teaspoon baking powder

2 tablespoons unsweetened cocoa powder

$^1/_2$ cup packed dark brown sugar

1 tablespoon vanilla extract

2 large eggs

$^1/_2$ cup chopped, toasted pecans

$^1/_4$ cup light rum

Confectioners' sugar

1. Preheat the oven to 350°F. Butter a 9 × 13-inch baking pan.

2. Place the chocolate and the butter into a large bowl, and place this bowl over a bowl of very hot water. Stir occasionally until both the chocolate and the butter are melted, then remove the mixture bowl from the bowl of hot water.

3. Stir the chocolate milk into the chocolate-butter mixture. Stir in the flour, baking powder, cocoa powder, brown sugar, vanilla, eggs, chopped pecans, and rum.

4. When all the ingredients are well incorporated, transfer the batter to the prepared pan. Bake for 25 to 30 minutes, or until the brownies spring back when pressed with a finger. Allow to cool completely.

5. Sprinkle the brownies with confectioners' sugar and cut them into squares.

223

VANILLA BEAN ICE CREAM

Once you've made this rich, creamy ice cream, transfer it to a Tupperware container or into a paper one-quart container. Store it in the freezer for up to one month.

SERVES 4 TO 6 | LEVEL: JUMP SHOT

7 large egg yolks	1 vanilla bean
¾ cup sugar	2 cups half-and-half
Pinch of kosher salt	1½ cups heavy cream

1. In a large mixing bowl, whisk the egg yolks with the sugar and salt.

2. Split the vanilla bean lengthwise and scrape out the seeds.

3. In a medium saucepan, combine the half-and-half, heavy cream, and vanilla bean seeds. Bring the mixture to a simmer. Whisking constantly, add the hot cream mixture to the egg mixture. Pour this back into the saucepan. Simmer, stirring constantly, until the mixture thickens.

4. Strain the mixture through a large sieve into a bowl and refrigerate, covered, until well chilled.

5. Transfer the mixture into an ice cream maker and freeze according to the manufacturer's directions.

SWEET POTATO PIE

In the South, this is a very traditional family dessert for the holidays. You can bake it a day ahead of time, and just before serving it, sprinkle the top with sugar and then use a little handheld kitchen torch to brown it. This gives the pie a nice crisp, crunchy topping.

SERVES 6 TO 8 | LEVEL: JUMP SHOT

4 medium sweet potatoes

4 tablespoons (¹/₂ stick) unsalted
   butter, softened

¹/₄ cup granulated sugar

³/₄ cup packed light brown sugar

1 tablespoon vanilla extract

1 teaspoon pumpkin pie spice

¹/₈ teaspoon ground cinnamon

¹/₈ teaspoon ground nutmeg

¹/₂ teaspoon kosher salt

³/₄ cup whole milk

1 teaspoon freshly squeezed lemon juice

2 large eggs, lightly beaten

1 9-inch unbaked pie shell

¹/₂ cup chopped pecans

For the topping:

¹/₂ cup granulated sugar

1. Preheat the oven to 350°F.

2. Place the sweet potatoes on a baking sheet and bake them for about 1 hour, or until they are soft. Allow them to cool them slightly. Remove and discard the skins, and transfer the potatoes to a medium bowl. Mash them slightly with a fork.

3. In a separate large bowl, using a handheld electric mixer set on medium speed, beat the butter, granulated sugar, and brown sugar for 1 minute. Add the vanilla, pumpkin pie spice, cinnamon, nutmeg, salt, milk, lemon juice, and eggs, and beat until well combined. Beat the cooked sweet potato into the egg-milk mixture.

4. Pour the sweet potato mixture into the pie shell, sprinkle with the chopped pecans, and bake for about 1 hour, or until the center of the pie is just set.

225

The pie is done when the center jiggles just a little when you move the pie pan back and forth. Remove the pie from the oven and let it cool on a rack.

5. When the pie is cool, sprinkle it with the sugar. Using a small handheld kitchen torch, brown the topping of the pie until the sugar caramelizes and is crisp and crunchy.

To save yourself some time, microwave the potatoes on a large plate until they are quite soft. This takes around 20 minutes in all, but you should turn them every 5 minutes. When the potatoes are cool enough to handle, split them in half, scoop out the flesh, and discard the skin.

"There is nothing like sweet potato pie during the holidays, and my wife, Alexis, makes an amazing one. The key to a great sweet potato pie is to use fresh, large sweet potatoes."

LEMON BARS

With a delicious filling over a crisp crust, these bars are a real crowd-pleaser. The simplest way to juice a lemon is to cut it in half and then use a handheld metal juicer, though you can also simply squeeze it to release the juice. Always juice lemons at room temperature. One medium lemon yields about 3 tablespoons of juice and 2 to 3 teaspoons of zest.

MAKES 12 BARS | LEVEL: JUMP SHOT

For the crust:

1 cup (2 sticks) unsalted butter, softened

2 cups all-purpose flour

1/2 cup confectioners' sugar

For the filling:

4 large eggs, at room temperature

2 1/2 cups granulated sugar

4 tablespoons all-purpose flour

1/4 cup freshly squeezed lemon juice

1 1/2 tablespoons freshly grated lemon zest

For the topping:

1/2 cup confectioners' sugar

12 fresh mint leaves

1. Preheat the oven to 350°F.

2. Make the crust: In a large mixing bowl, with a handheld electric mixer set on medium speed, beat the butter with the flour and the confectioners' sugar. When the ingredients are well incorporated, press the dough evenly into a 9 × 13-inch baking pan. Bake the crust for about 15 minutes or until it is golden. Allow the crust to cool slightly.

3. Make the filling: In a medium mixing bowl, beat the eggs, sugar, flour, lemon juice, and lemon zest until well blended. Pour the filling over the crust. Return the baking pan to the oven and bake the bars for about 25 minutes or until the topping is set and the crust is golden brown.

4. Remove the pan from the oven and allow it to cool slightly. Sprinkle it with the confectioners' sugar, then cut the pan into 12 bars and top each one with a mint leaf.

RED VELVET SWIRL CHEESECAKE

Your cheesecake will be at its creamiest, richest best if you keep these pointers in mind. Make sure your cream cheese is at room temperature. Don't cheat on this one (and don't use the microwave to warm up the cream cheese!) or you'll wind up with a lumpy cheesecake. Beat the batter until it's very smooth before adding the eggs, and once the eggs have been added, take care to beat just until well incorporated. Beating air into the cheesecake allows it to puff up as it bakes. If it has too much air beaten into it, it may crack once it's out of the oven.

SERVES 12 | LEVEL: JUMP SHOT

For the crust:

1¹/₂ cups finely crushed graham cracker crumbs (about 9 graham crackers)

3 tablespoons sugar

6 tablespoons butter, melted

Butter to coat the springform pan

For the filling:

1 ounce bittersweet or semi-sweet chocolate, chopped

¹/₂ tablespoon unsalted butter, softened

3 8-ounce packages cream cheese, at room temperature

1 cup sugar

1 teaspoon vanilla extract

3 large eggs

1 to 2 teaspoons red food coloring (the amount varies depending on how red you want the cake to be)

1. Preheat the oven to 300° F.

2. To prepare the crust: In a small mixing bowl, thoroughly mix the graham cracker crumbs, sugar, and melted butter. Press firmly onto the bottom (and up the sides, if you want) of a lightly buttered 8-inch springform pan.

229

3. To prepare the filling: Partially melt the chopped chocolate and butter together in the microwave on low (or in a double boiler on the stovetop). Stir until completely melted. Set aside.

4. In a large mixing bowl, beat the cream cheese until smooth; add the sugar and the vanilla extract, and beat until completely incorporated, scraping the sides of the bowl frequently. Add the eggs all at once and beat *just* until the eggs are incorporated—no more than about 10 seconds.

5. Remove about $1/2$ cup of the batter to a small mixing bowl, and fold in the melted chocolate mixture and the red food coloring just until completely incorporated.

6. Pour the white batter into the prepared springform pan, and spoon the red batter in a few dollops over the top. Using a knife, gently make a few swirled patterns in the batter. If you swirl too much, you'll lose the patterns you've created.

7. Bake the cake for 1 hour, or until the center no longer jiggles when the pan is gently moved. Avoid checking the cake until it's been in the oven for 1 hour, or it may crack when removed from the oven.

8. Remove the cake from the oven and let it cool on a wire rack. After 10 minutes, gently run a knife around the edges of the pan to help release the crust. Let the cheesecake sit at room temperature for 1 hour. Refrigerate the cake for at least 8 hours or overnight. When you're ready to serve, release the springform and slice the cake with a warm knife.

231

TIME OUT FOR FAMILY

....

"AMAR'E

Where I was born and mostly raised, in Lake Wales, Florida, which is near Orlando, my aunts and my mother cooked traditional Southern fare. Like Max's mother, my mother is a good cook, though it was really more my aunt Dilly who made so many of the memorable dishes we loved as kids. We moved around a lot when I was growing up, so I really valued the times that we sat down as a family and ate a meal together.

In the South, food is always front, center, and everywhere. We ate fruits and vegetables that were grown right where we lived. As kids, we'd go to my grandfather's house and pick peaches from his tree, and eat them with lots of ice cream. My fondest food memories are of collard greens, yams, and delicious smoked turkey legs, and there was always a pot of greens on the stove on Sunday when I was growing up. All my friends and extended family would come over just to get a plate of my aunt's greens.

Since food was so important in my family when I was growing up, I want to pass along a love of good food to my children. When Alexis and I sit down with our kids for a meal, stories are shared, and we eat food made from family recipes that are steeped in tradition. I love these times.

I want to impart to my children the importance of being conscientious eaters and of knowing what they are eating and where the food comes from so they can make an informed decision about what to eat.

Not only do I want my children to appreciate the food they eat, I want them to learn how to prepare it themselves. Already they're learning how to make their own breakfasts, lunches, and snacks. I like to think I am their inspiration, since they watch me cooking on the weekends.

One of our favorite dishes to make as a family is pizza. Everything is prepared from scratch, including the dough, and then we all add our toppings. Sometimes we can get pretty creative! It's a ton of fun, and always exciting to create something with your children. Then we all sit down together to eat it. My children are learning that food is meant to be shared, and that mealtime is meant to draw the family close.

MAX

My mom's side of the family is from the Bahamas and my grandmother, my aunts, and my mom have kept their nation's rich culinary traditions close at hand. Just as they did while I was growing up, they still cook up Bahamian specialties and

traditional Southern fare for every special occasion. I learned so much by watching them, and my Bahamian roots are definitely on display in my cooking, with plenty of fun flavors—lots of color, lots of herbs, and a wide variety of spices.

Growing up in Florida, I was lucky enough to eat guava, lobster, and red snapper on a regular basis. Besides fresh fish, my mother also used to make us comfort food like Stew Chicken (page 247), which is a homey dish that's great over rice or mashed potatoes. My mother's Country Fried Steak (page 239) is legendary. She also makes amazing conch salad and conch fritters.

My mom and I still cook a lot together, either when I go to her house or when she comes into town. Occasionally, we have Sunday "fun days," when she is visiting, and when my family comes over, my mom and I cook up a storm. She is an amazing cook, so when we are together, it's just great food.

One of the best parts of showing Amar'e how to cook is seeing him pass along his enthusiasm and passion for good, healthy food to his children. It's so important that they are learning from their dad that real food is what matters. Amar'e's love of cooking is obviously contagious, since his kids are curious and creative in the kitchen. They just can't wait to get in there with us and get their hands into the food.

FULL COURT PRESS

Cooking for friends and family means opening up your heart, sharing your cooking with love, and putting yourself out there by making everyone feel special. Because when you throw a party, be it an elegant soiree for sixty or an intimate supper for six, you want your guests to have more than good food. You want them to kick back, relax, have fun, and feel at home.

In order for your guests to be relaxed and have fun, you need to do the same. Approach entertaining with a positive and laid back attitude. Make it all seem easy, and you may be surprised that, after a while, it really does seem reasonably stress-free. Keep a smile on your face, act confident and in control, and you'll pull off a party with panache.

Here's how to have the best party ever.

• Plan in advance (whenever possible). Of course there will be times when unexpected company drops in and winds up staying for dinner. But most of the time, you've got enough advance notice that you can sit down and come up with a workable menu. By workable, this means that not every dish on the menu should be complicated and need a lot of last minute attention. If you do one labor-intensive dish that requires your time in the kitchen, bal-

237

ance it out with other dishes that you can prepare ahead of time and leave out until serving time or reheat when it's time to eat.

•Mix it up. Go rogue by coming up with the unexpected, so your guests get some little surprises, whether this means a fun cocktail, an unexpected garnish on an entree, a mash up of flavors in a flatbread, or a twist on a dessert classic.

•Have some food set out as soon as guests arrive. Steak bites or burger bites, or another beef option, are great to have on hand for when guests arrive.

•For a good vibe, have some great music playing. It loosens everything up and gets everyone in a good, fun mood. Bob Marley or some other reggae music is great for parties.

•Accept that everything won't be perfect. Sometimes, even with the most carefully laid plans, things can and do go wrong. Food burns in the pot, soup gets oversalted, vegetables turn mushy, or there's not quite enough of a particular dish. Relax and smile. Nobody's perfect and your guests will love you no matter what. And since every cooking experience is a learning experience, you will just keep getting better and better.

238

COUNTRY FRIED STEAK

This recipe changes up the classic version of a country fried steak and takes it to the next level with a great coating on the steak.

SERVES 6 | LEVEL: JUMP SHOT

2 cups all-purpose flour

Kosher salt and freshly ground black
    pepper to taste

3 tablespoons garlic powder

1 tablespoon mild paprika

3 large eggs

1 cup buttermilk

2$^{1}/_{2}$ cups extra-virgin olive oil

6 6-ounce rib eye steaks

1. In a large bowl, combine the flour, salt, pepper, garlic powder, and paprika. In a medium bowl, lightly beat the eggs. Pour the buttermilk into another medium bowl.

2. Preheat a large sauté pan over medium-high heat for 1 minute. Pour the olive oil into the pan.

3. Dip each steak into buttermilk and then into the seasoned flour. Shake off any excess flour. Dip each steak into the beaten egg and then into the seasoned flour again.

4. Carefully transfer the steaks to the sauté pan and cook until the coating is caramelized and the steaks are cooked to medium, about 2 to 3 minutes per side.

COLLARD GREENS WITH BRAISED TURKEY LEGS

You can treat collard greens the same way as kale in terms of how to clean and cut them. And for this dish, it's great to follow the tradition of adding a rutabaga for extra crunchiness. If you don't have rutabagas, parsnips work well, too. Add one rutabaga or parsnip, cut up, when you add the collard greens. Buy the turkey legs in any supermarket—both fresh and frozen work.

SERVES 6 TO 8 | LEVEL: JUMP SHOT

3 quarts Chicken Stock, plus more as needed (page 27)

3 smoked turkey legs (thawed, if frozen)

4 bunches fresh collard greens, washed thoroughly

2 large yellow onions, chopped

3 tablespoons seasoned salt

1 tablespoon freshly ground black pepper

2 tablespoons garlic powder

$1/4$ cup hot sauce

3 tablespoons sugar

1. In a 10-quart stockpot, bring the chicken stock to a boil. Add the smoked turkey legs and cook on medium while you prepare the greens.

2. Remove the stems from the collard greens. Stack the leaves, roll them up, and cut them in half.

3. Add the collard greens and the chopped onion to the stockpot. Reduce the heat to a simmer. Sprinkle the greens with the seasoned salt, pepper, garlic powder, hot sauce, and sugar. Cover the stockpot and simmer for about 1 hour, or until the collard greens are tender. If the liquid starts to evaporate, add more chicken stock.

" Wow! When I was growing up, my aunt had a pot of greens on the stove every Sunday. All my friends and family would come over just to get a plate. When my aunt met Chef Max, he made some greens; and when she tasted them, she laughed and said to him, 'Now I see why Amar'e needs you!'"

241

PIGEON PEAS AND RICE

This traditional Bahamian dish, somewhat similar to Jamaican rice and peas, can be served with just about any meat, but it is especially good with chicken and ribs.

SERVES 6 | LEVEL: JUMP SHOT

1/2 large yellow onion, chopped

1 tablespoon tomato paste

1/4 cup extra-virgin olive oil

2 tablespoons stemmed, chopped fresh thyme

1 cup uncooked long grain parboiled white rice (such as Uncle Ben's)

1 cup pigeon peas

2 cups Chicken Stock (page 27)

1. In a large skillet, sauté the onion and the tomato paste in the olive oil for 2 to 3 minutes, or until the onion softens. Stir in the thyme.

2. Stir in the rice, pigeon peas, and chicken stock. Bring to a boil, reduce the heat, and simmer, covered, for about 15 minutes or until the rice and the peas are tender.

3. Transfer to a serving dish and serve hot.

BAKED SWEET POTATO "FRIES"

This is a great dish to make for the kids. They think it is like eating potato chips, but it is a lot healthier since the potatoes aren't fried. It's got good crunch to it, and the rosemary really brings out the flavor.

SERVES 6 TO 8 | LEVEL: LAYUP

8 sweet potatoes

¼ cup extra-virgin olive oil

2 sprigs chopped fresh rosemary

1 teaspoon kosher salt, or to taste

Freshly ground black pepper to taste

1. Preheat the oven to 350°F.

2. Peel the potatoes, if desired. Cut them into ½-inch-thick wedges. Place the potato wedges into a large bowl of cool water and allow them to soak for about 20 minutes.

3. Pat the potato wedges dry with paper towels. Toss them with the olive oil and the rosemary. Arrange the potato wedges in a single layer on a parchment-lined baking sheet. Bake them for about 25 minutes, then turn over the wedges, using a large spatula.

4. Continue to bake the fries for another 15 minutes or until they are soft inside and crispy on the outside. Remove the fries from the oven and sprinkle them with the salt and with pepper to taste.

BUTTERMILK FRIED CHICKEN

This is a great Sunday-night dinner. The larger pieces of chicken, such as the breast or large thighs, will take a little longer to cook. If they start to darken too much in the hot oil, place into a preheated, 350°F oven until they are thoroughly cooked.

SERVES 6 TO 8 | LEVEL: JUMP SHOT

4 pounds chicken pieces (drumsticks, thighs, wings, and breast)

Kosher salt to taste

Freshly ground black pepper to taste, plus 1 tablespoon pepper for the coating

2 cups buttermilk

6 cups all-purpose flour

3 tablespoons garlic powder

3 tablespoons onion powder

3 tablespoons mild paprika

10 cups vegetable oil

1. Place the chicken in a large bowl. Season it with salt and pepper to taste. Pour the buttermilk over the chicken, cover the bowl with plastic wrap, and refrigerate it for about 4 hours. Rotate the chicken pieces a couple of times so all the pieces willl be evenly marinated in the buttermilk.

2. When you are ready to fry the chicken, combine the flour, garlic powder, onion powder, 1 tablespoon pepper, and paprika in a very large resealable

plastic bag. Place the chicken, a few pieces at a time, in the bag and shake until they are well-coated with the seasoned flour. Repeat with the remaining chicken.

3. In a very large, heavy cast iron skillet, heat the oil over medium heat until it reaches 350°F. Fry the chicken a few pieces at a time, being careful not to overcrowd the pan, for 12 to 15 minutes or until it is golden brown and thoroughly done.

4. As you remove the chicken from the saucepan, place it on a large plate on layers of paper towels to remove any excess oil.

" This is my Sunday special. Chef and I came up with the idea of Soul Food Sundays, and when we have soul food on that day, fried chicken has to be on the menu. I have mastered this recipe so I can give Chef a hand. We normally invite a few friends over and I act as executive chef and Chef Max is my sous chef (LOL)."

246

STEW CHICKEN

You can make this on top of the stove, or just put everything into the slow cooker and let it go. If you use a slow cooker, brown the meat and vegetables first and then cook it on low for about 4 hours or until done. Serve this in large bowls with rice.

SERVES 4 TO 6 | LEVEL: LAYUP

4 pounds chicken wings and drumsticks

Kosher salt and freshly ground black pepper to taste

3 tablespoons garlic powder

2 cups all-purpose flour

3/4 cup extra-virgin olive oil

4 large red potatoes, diced

1/4 pound cremini mushrooms, sliced

1 large yellow onion, chopped

3 garlic cloves, minced

2 carrots, chopped

1 celery stalk, chopped

2 cups Chicken Stock (page 27)

3 tablespoons tomato paste

1 bunch fresh parsley, stemmed and chopped

2 tablespoons chopped fresh thyme

1/4 cup heavy cream

1. Season the chicken with salt, pepper, and garlic powder. Toss the chicken with the flour.

2. In a large heavy skillet, heat the olive oil over medium heat and cook the chicken for 3 minutes on each side, or until it is browned. Pour off half the fat. Add the potatoes, mushrooms, onion, garlic, carrots, and celery. Cook on medium for 15 minutes or until all the vegetables are softened but not mushy. They should still be al dente.

3. Stir in the chicken stock, tomato paste, parsley, and thyme. Cook, covered, on medium heat for 35 minutes or until the chicken is cooked and the vegetables are tender but al dente. Stir in the heavy cream.

SOUTHERN MAC-N-CHEESE

It's important to watch this dish carefully and not overbake it. You want the top to be crispy and browned but the interior to be moist and creamy. You might even want to add a little extra Colby cheese to the top of the dish before baking this.

SERVES 8 TO 10 | LEVEL: JUMP SHOT

Butter for greasing the baking pan

2 tablespoons kosher salt

2 boxes (16 ounces) uncooked elbow macaroni

1 1/2 cups shredded mild cheddar cheese

1 cup shredded smoked cheddar cheese

1 cup shredded mozzarella cheese

2 cups cubed mild cheddar cheese

2 large eggs

3 cups half-and-half

2 tablespoons dried parsley

1 teaspoon freshly ground black pepper

2 tablespoons garlic powder

2 tablespoons onion powder

1 tablespoon seasoned salt

1. Preheat the oven to 350°F.

2. Bring a 6-quart stockpot of water to a boil. Add 1 tablespoon of the kosher salt. Add the macaroni, and cook it according to the package directions. Drain the macaroni but do not rinse it. Transfer the macaroni to a large bowl.

3. Stir in 1 cup of the mild cheddar, the smoked cheddar, mozzarella, mild cheddar, and eggs. Add the half-and-half, parsley, black pepper, the remaining 1 tablespoon kosher salt, garlic powder, onion powder, and seasoned salt. Stir until the macaroni is evenly coated with cheese and the cheese is starting to melt.

4. Transfer the macaroni to a deep buttered 9 × 13-inch baking dish. Evenly sprinkle with the remaining 1/2 cup cheddar. Bake the macaroni, uncovered, for 15 minutes or until the top is golden and bubbly.

249

"I spent many days in the kitchen as a child watching my grandmom in Detroit put her foot in the macaroni and cheese," says Max. "That's an expression that means she did a great job on it. This is no ordinary macaroni and cheese, but a richer, spicier version inspired by my grandmom. The smoked cheddar gives it an especially nice kick."

" This is one of my favorite comfort foods. I try not to eat it as much as I would like to as I am trying to keep my *GQ* figure, but I must say it is one of my guilty pleasures."

CRISPY CORNMEAL-BATTERED FISH

This is a great dish to serve family-style, although you also could serve it on a buffet with rice. It's good with any type of white fish—red snapper is my favorite, but you could substitute cod.

SERVES 4 | LEVEL: JUMP SHOT

8 3-ounce red snapper fillets

3 tablespoons Old Bay Seasoning

Freshly ground black pepper

2 tablespoons garlic powder

2 tablespoons onion powder

1 cup fine yellow cornmeal

2 cups all-purpose flour

4 large eggs

6 cups vegetable oil

3 lemons

1. Season the snapper on both sides with the Old Bay Seasoning, black pepper, garlic powder, and onion powder.

2. In a medium bowl, combine the cornmeal with the flour. In a second bowl, lightly beat the eggs.

3. In a very large, heavy cast iron skillet or a deep fryer, heat the oil over medium heat until it reaches 350°F. Dip the snapper into the cornmeal mixture, then into the egg mixture, and then back into the cornmeal mixture. Using a slotted spoon or large spatula, transfer the pieces of snapper into the hot oil. Do not crowd the pan. Fry the snapper for 3 to 5 minutes, turning once halfway through the cooking. Remove the fish from the hot oil when it is golden brown and crisp on the outside and opaque on the inside.

4. Halve 1 lemon. Cut the others into wedges. Squeeze the juice from the halved lemon over the snapper fillets. Garnish the snapper fillets with the lemon wedges.

"This is another Soul Food Sunday favorite. The key to this recipe is to make sure it's breaded correctly so it can get nice and crispy. Freshly squeezed lemons are also important. I make sure Chef fries a few extra just for me because it's one of my favorites."

253

FISH AND GRITS

Fish and grits is a natural pairing in Southern cooking. While it is traditional to use catfish, this dish is delicious with snapper, flounder, or whiting.

SERVES 6 | LEVEL: LAYUP

6 3-ounce catfish fillets

2 tablespoons mild paprika

2 tablespoons garlic powder

3 tablespoons onion powder

Kosher salt and freshly ground black
  pepper to taste

1 teaspoon cayenne pepper

1 teaspoon fresh oregano

3 cups all-purpose flour

6 cups vegetable oil

5 cups Chicken Stock (page 27)

2 cups quick-cooking grits

2 tablespoons unsalted butter

1 cup shredded mild cheddar cheese

1 tablespoon chopped fresh chives (or
  parsley) as a garnish

1. Season the fillets with the paprika, garlic powder, onion powder, salt, 1 teaspoon black pepper, cayenne pepper, and oregano. Scoop the flour onto a plate. Coat the fish with the flour, turning so that all sides are coated.

2. In a large, heavy cast iron skillet or fryer, heat the oil over medium heat until it reaches 350°F. Place the fish fillets in the hot oil, being careful not to overcrowd the pan. Fry the fillets for 3 to 5 minutes, carefully flipping once with a spatula, until they are golden brown. Repeat until all the fish is fried.

3. Meanwhile, bring the chicken stock to a boil in a large saucepan. Whisk in the grits, reduce the heat to a simmer, and cook for 10 to 15 minutes or until the stock is completely absorbed. You may need to add a little extra stock or water if the liquid evaporates before the grits are fully cooked.

4. Remove the grits from the heat and add salt and pepper to taste, along with the cheese.

5. Spoon some grits onto each plate, top with a piece of fish, and garnish with the chives.

FRIED FISH AND CREAMY POLENTA

Using polenta in place of grits gives this dish extra flavor and color. Sole works well because it is firm and yet just soft enough to be appealing, but you also could use tilapia, snapper, or grouper.

SERVES 4 | LEVEL: JUMP SHOT

$^1/_2$ cup whole milk

1 tablespoon freshly squeezed lemon juice

8 3-ounce sole fillets

2 cups vegetable oil

$^1/_3$ cup coarse yellow cornmeal

$^1/_3$ cup all-purpose flour

1 teaspoon mild paprika

$^1/_2$ teaspoon freshly ground black pepper

$^1/_2$ teaspoon kosher salt

$^1/_2$ teaspoon garlic powder

$^1/_2$ teaspoon dried thyme

$^1/_8$ teaspoon cayenne pepper

Creamy Polenta (recipe follows)

1. In a medium bowl, combine the milk and lemon juice. Add the sole fillets. Set them aside to marinate for about 5 minutes.

2. In a large, heavy skillet over medium heat, heat the oil until it is 350°F.

3. In a shallow bowl, stir together the cornmeal and flour. Season it with the paprika, black pepper, salt, garlic powder, thyme, and cayenne pepper. Remove the fish fillets from the milk mixture and shake them to remove excess moisture. Roll each fillet in the cornmeal mixture.

4. Carefully add the fish fillets to the skillet, making sure they are in a single layer. Fry them for about 2 minutes on each side, or until golden brown. If your skillet isn't large enough to hold the fish in a single layer, fry them in two batches. Remove the finished fillets to a paper towel–lined plate to drain. Serve the fish with Creamy Polenta.

255

"Totally out of the box for me. I had never heard of polenta and I thought it was grits with food coloring. I thought Chef Max was crazy. Now it is one of my favorites."

CREAMY POLENTA

When preparing polenta, be sure to add the cornmeal to the water or stock in a slow stream, whisking constantly, so that no lumps form. You can pretty much use any grind of cornmeal (coarse, medium, or fine) when making polenta. The cooking time varies depending on whether you use coarse, fine, or medium cornmeal.

SERVES 6 TO 8 | LEVEL: LAYUP

4 cups Chicken Stock (page 27)

1 teaspoon kosher salt

$^1/_2$ teaspoon freshly ground black pepper

2 cups polenta

4 tablespoons unsalted butter

2 ounces sharp cheddar cheese, shredded

$^1/_4$ cup snipped fresh chives

$^1/_4$ cup chopped tomato

1. In a large, heavy saucepan, combine the stock, salt, and pepper. Bring to a boil over medium-high heat. Gradually add the polenta, whisking constantly. Once all the polenta has been incorporated, reduce the heat to low and cover the pot.

2. Cook on low, whisking every few minutes to prevent the polenta from sticking or forming lumps and making sure to get into the corners of the pot. Simmer the polenta for 20 to 25 minutes, or until creamy. Remove from the heat and whisk in the butter.

3. Once the butter is incorporated, gradually stir in the cheese a little at a time. Spoon into a large serving bowl, top with the chives and tomato, and serve immediately with the fried fish.

HOMEMADE BAGEL BITES

So much better than the frozen kind, these make a great snack. For kids who are just starting to cook, this is a perfect dish to make with them. You'll find jars of pizza sauce in the supermarket in the pasta aisle, adjacent to the jars of spaghetti sauce.

MAKES 6 | LEVEL: LAYUP

1 1/2 cups pizza sauce

3 mini bagels, halved

2 cups grated mozzarella cheese

1 cup turkey pepperoni slices

1 tablespoon garlic powder

1 tablespoon Italian seasoning

1 cup grated Parmesan cheese

4 fresh basil leaves, chopped

1. Preheat the oven to 350°F.

2. Cover a large baking sheet with foil and spray it with nonstick cooking spray.

3. Spread each bagel half with a layer of pizza sauce. Sprinkle each one with some mozzarella cheese and a few pieces of pepperoni. Arrange the bagel bites on the prepared baking sheet.

4. Season each bagel bite with a little garlic powder and Italian seasoning.

5. Bake the bagel bites for 8 to 10 minutes, or until the cheese is melted and the sauce is very hot. Remove the bagel bites from the oven and sprinkle each one with a little Parmesan cheese and some chopped basil.

259

FRIED OKRA

Okra, a favorite ingredient in gumbo, can also be braised, baked, or fried. In the fast-food chicken restaurants in Florida, fried okra is often on the menu. You can serve this for lunch or as an appetizer. It's especially good in the summer.

SERVES 6 | LEVEL: JUMP SHOT

3 large eggs

1 pound fresh okra (whole)

2 cups all-purpose flour

1 cup fine yellow cornmeal

2 teaspoons mild paprika

Kosher salt and freshly ground black pepper to taste

5 cups vegetable oil

1. In a medium bowl, lightly whisk the eggs. Add the okra and stir until it is well coated with the beaten egg.

2. In a resealable plastic bag, combine the flour, cornmeal, paprika, salt, and pepper. Shake well.

3. In a large, deep frying pan, heat the oil over medium heat to 350°F.

4. Place the okra, a few pieces at a time, into the resealable plastic bag and shake until the okra is completely coated with the flour mixture. Carefully transfer the okra to the hot oil and cook over medium for about 5 minutes or until golden brown. Remove the okra to a paper towel–lined plate. Repeat this process with the remaining okra.

260

BRAISED KALE WITH GARLICKY TURNIPS

Kale is a great source of vitamins and other nutrients, and combining it with turnips seems to bring out the best flavor in both vegetables. When choosing turnips, always choose the smaller ones, which are sweeter and more delicate than the older ones.

SERVES 6 | LEVEL: LAYUP

$1/4$ cup extra-virgin olive oil

$1/2$ large yellow onion, diced

1 teaspoon crushed red pepper flakes

2 small turnips, peeled and cubed

2 garlic cloves, minced

Kosher salt and freshly ground black
  pepper to taste

1 cup Chicken Stock (page 27),
  and more as needed

3 pounds kale, torn, with stems removed

$1/4$ cup apple cider vinegar

$1/2$ cup (1 stick) unsalted butter

1. Heat the olive oil over medium heat in a large, heavy saucepan. Add the onion and red pepper flakes, and sauté for 3 to 5 minutes or until the onion softens.

2. Add the cubed turnip, garlic, salt, pepper, and chicken stock. Bring to a boil.

3. Add the kale, reduce the heat to low, and cook, stirring often, for about 25 minutes. If the mixture starts to look dry, add a little more stock. When done, the kale should be wilted but still firm to the bite. The color will be deep green.

4. Season the vegetables with additional salt and pepper, as needed. Transfer to a serving bowl, drizzle with the vinegar, and stir in the butter until it melts.

"I have to be honest. I never had kale or turnips before I met Chef Max. The first time he served me kale, I gave him the evil eye, but after I tasted this dish, my feelings for kale changed. Now I love it. I even love kale salad."

264

TRAIL MIX

This is a great snack for kids, who can put it in a resealable plastic bag and take it to sports practices. It will keep for a couple of weeks at room temperature.

MAKES 6 CUPS | LEVEL: LAYUP

1 cup shelled almonds

1 cup shelled cashews

1 cup shelled pecans

$^1/_2$ cup dried chopped mango

1 cup dried cherries

1 cup raisins

1 cup sunflower seeds

1 tablespoon sea salt

1 teaspoon ground cinnamon

1 tablespoon extra-virgin olive oil

1. In a large bowl, combine the almonds, cashews, pecans, dried mango, dried cherries, raisins, sunflower seeds, sea salt, cinnamon, and olive oil.

2. Mix thoroughly. Store in an airtight container.

CORN MUFFINS

Every grandmother in the South has a great recipe for corn muffins that are made ahead and kept around the house. You could serve these at breakfast or dinner, as they go well with collard greens, braised kale, soups, and stews.

MAKES 24 MUFFINS | LEVEL: LAYUP

2 cups fine yellow cornmeal

1 cup all-purpose flour

2 tablespoons baking powder

$1/2$ teaspoon baking soda

1 teaspoon kosher salt

2 tablespoons sugar

3 large eggs

1 cup buttermilk

1 small can creamed corn

4 tablespoons unsalted butter, softened, plus more for the tops of the muffins

1. Preheat the oven to 350°F.

2. Line two muffin tins with paper muffin cups.

3. In a large bowl, combine the cornmeal, flour, baking powder, baking soda, salt, and sugar.

4. In another large bowl, whisk the eggs with the buttermilk. Stir in the creamed corn and the softened butter. Stir the wet ingredients into the dry ingredients, and continue to stir just until blended.

5. Spoon the batter into the muffin tins. Bake for 20 to 25 minutes, or until the tops of the muffins are golden brown and a toothpick inserted into the center of each one comes out clean. Top each muffin with a little butter while still warm.

FLUFF SANDWICHES WITH BANANAS AND NUTELLA (TURTLE SANDWICHES)

This is a sweet favorite that's hard for anyone to resist, and it's ready in minutes.

MAKES 6 SANDWICHES | LEVEL: LAYUP

6 slices whole-wheat bread

$^1/_4$ cup peanut butter

1 cup Marshmallow Fluff

$^1/_2$ cup jelly (your favorite kind)

1 cup Nutella

2 bananas, sliced

1. Toast the bread.

2. For each sandwich, spread 1 slice of toast with a thin layer of peanut butter. Top with a thin layer of Marshmallow Fluff and a thin layer of jelly. Spread a layer of Nutella on a second slice of toast.

3. Arrange a layer of banana slices over the Nutella. Make a sandwich with the two slices of toast; cut it in half. Repeat with the remaining toast.

CHICKEN MEATBALLS WITH TERIYAKI GLAZE

If you're in the mood for an Asian-flavored entrée, try this dish, and feel free to sub in ground turkey for the ground chicken. It's excellent over pasta or rice.

SERVES 8 TO 10 | LEVEL: JUMP SHOT

For the meatballs:

3 pounds ground chicken

4 large eggs

2 cups bread crumbs

$^1/_2$ cup stemmed, chopped fresh cilantro

$^1/_4$ cup Worcestershire sauce

Kosher salt and freshly ground pepper to taste

For the teriyaki glaze:

1 cup pineapple juice

$^1/_2$ cup soy sauce

$^1/_2$ cup loose light brown sugar

2 tablespoons cornstarch

2 tablespoons grated fresh ginger

2 garlic cloves, finely minced

1. Preheat the oven to 350°F.

2. In a large bowl, combine the ground chicken, eggs, bread crumbs, cilantro, Worcestershire sauce, salt, and pepper. Mix well with your hands. Roll the meat mixture into golf ball–sized meatballs and place them on a nonstick baking sheet.

3. Bake the meatballs for about 20 minutes, or until they are thoroughly cooked.

4. Meanwhile, in a large saucepan, combine the pineapple juice, soy sauce, brown sugar, cornstarch, ginger, and garlic. Whisking constantly, cook the sauce over medium heat until it is thick and bubbly. Brush the glaze on the meatballs during the last 5 minutes of baking.

PRIME STEAK QUESADILLAS

Quesadillas traditionally are made with flour tortillas that are filled with cooked vegetables or meat, folded in half, and toasted or broiled until crisp. This one is a little different in that the filling (tender steak, shredded cheese, and sautéed portobellos) is spooned onto a tortilla. Another tortilla is placed on top, and the quesadilla is cooked in a grill pan until crisp.

SERVES 6 | LEVEL: JUMP SHOT

3 6-ounce skirt steaks

Kosher salt and freshly ground black pepper to taste

$\frac{1}{4}$ cup extra-virgin olive oil

2 portobello mushrooms, sliced

1 green bell pepper, cored, seeded, and sliced

$\frac{1}{2}$ large red onion, sliced

6 12-inch flour tortillas

1 cup shredded pepper jack cheese

1 cup mild or sharp cheddar cheese

1 cup sour cream

1 bunch fresh cilantro, stemmed and chopped

1. Season the steaks with salt and pepper.

2. Heat a medium sauté pan over medium heat for 1 minute. Add half the olive oil and when it sizzles, add the portobello mushroom, bell pepper, and red onion. Sauté the vegetables for 1 minute or until they start to look caramelized.

3. Preheat a large sauté pan over medium heat for 1 minute. Add the remaining olive oil. When it sizzles, add the steaks. Cook, turning once, for 2 to 3 minutes per side or until browned but still rare.

4. Transfer the steaks to a cutting board and allow them to sit for about 3 minutes. Slice the steaks into thin strips.

5. Preheat a large grill pan over medium heat for 1 minute. Arrange 2 tortillas in the grill pan and sprinkle them with the pepper jack cheese. Top

271

with the sliced steak and the sautéed vegetables. Sprinkle with the cheddar cheese, and top with another tortilla. Cook, pressing down, until the cheese is melted and the bottom tortilla is crisp. Flip over and continue to cook for another minute or until the bottom tortilla is crisp.

6. Let the quesadillas cool for a minute before cutting them into quarters. Garnish with a dollop of sour cream and some cilantro.

GRILLED HONEY GARLIC CHICKEN WINGS

Kids simply love eating this dish as a main course, but it's also great to serve at parties. While you can make it easily on an outdoor grill, this dish can be made in your kitchen, too, if you have a grill pan.

SERVES 8 TO 10 | LEVEL: JUMP SHOT

1/2 cup honey

1/4 cup soy sauce

4 garlic cloves, chopped

1/4 cup loose light brown sugar

Juice of 2 lemons

1/4 cup extra-virgin olive oil

1 tablespoon mild paprika

1 bunch fresh cilantro, stemmed and chopped

6 1/2 pounds chicken wings

Kosher salt and freshly ground black pepper to taste

1. Preheat a large grill to medium for about 15 minutes.

2. In a small bowl, whisk the honey, soy sauce, garlic, brown sugar, lemon juice, and olive oil. Divide the marinade between 2 bowls.

3. Stir the paprika and half the cilantro into one bowl of marinade. Marinate the chicken in this for about 30 minutes or overnight. Set aside the other bowl of marinade.

4. Remove the chicken wings from the bowl and discard the marinade. Place the chicken wings on the grill, and grill them for 10 to 12 minutes or until they are thoroughly cooked, flipping them over once and brushing them with the reserved marinade.

5. Transfer the chicken wings to a serving platter, brush with a little of the reserved marinade, and sprinkle them with the remaining chopped cilantro.

273

BAKED BRIE

When friends come over to visit, this makes a perfect snack to set out with drinks. The perfect accompaniment is warm French bread.

SERVES 6 TO 8 | LEVEL: LAYUP

2 8-ounce rounds of Brie

1 cup honey

3 garlic cloves, minced

Warm French bread or your favorite crackers, for serving

1. Preheat the oven to 350°F.

2. Arrange the rounds of Brie on a large baking sheet.

3. In a small bowl, combine the honey with the minced garlic. Drizzle the Brie with the honey and bake for 5 minutes, or until the Brie is melted and oozing.

4. Serve immediately, with the French bread or the crackers.

As teacher and student, we shared a goal while writing this book: to teach you all the techniques you need for success in the kitchen and to provide you with a fun, unique collection of recipes to nourish you from morning right on through to the evening. Whether you are a vegetarian who cooks for one, a parent always looking for dishes to tempt your picky eater, or a party host who frequently entertains a houseful, we hope that this book is a source of delicious inspiration.

Whether you've cooked your way through our book from start to finish or have whipped up just a few dishes so far, we hope that you have enjoyed what you've tasted. If you have stepped away from the stove with a smile on your face after preparing our recipes, we feel grateful. It is our hope that you have happily shared these dishes with those you love.

Bonding over food with family and friends is one of life's great joys, and we hope this book will always inspire you to prepare great meals that will offer comfort and sustenance to those who are close to you.

277

AMAR'E

I'd like to thank Alexis Stoudemire, my wife, and my children, Ar'e, Amar'e Jr., Assata, and Alijah Stoudemire.

MAX:

Team Chef Max—I would like to thank Hnede Lamphey, Aisha Shackerford, Chef Richard Roberts, Chef Nichole Mooney, Chef Troy Tingley, Chef Rudy Straker (NYC), Chef Rudy Pondexter (MIA), Tylesis Nelson. You have all truly made my life a lot easier. You have been loyal and been the best support system a chef could ask for, in all my moments. Many thanks to Rosemary Black for being a wonderful cowriter. It has been a short but sweet ride. Thanks for your professionalism and experience. Stacey Glick, our literary agent, wow! I remember the first meeting we had in your office. It was like a dream come true. Thanks for allowing my talents to be illustrated on paper.

AM Media Group—Americk Lewis, Nicholas Sosin, and Lonut Vacar: guys, I'm so happy you all were part of this experience. It truly made my life easier shooting

279

the pictures of the book and my day-to-day life. We have seen each other's lives and companies grow, and it has been amazing. Thanks so much.

Rebecca Bent—thanks so much for the introduction to Stacey. This wouldn't be a book if it weren't for you. Thanks for the amazing support and all the great advice you have given me over the years. Wow! Thank you; I owe you.

Bakehouse—Chef Philip, thanks for opening up your door to shoot so many of the amazing recipes and allowing me to take book meetings in your restaurant (laughter). Mixologist Louie Estrada, my man!!!!!! Thanks so much; it was great creating some wonderful cocktails with you that will always be my favorites, and now I'm sure the world will be enjoying them as well.

To the fans—to everyone who has been a fan of Chef Max and who rocked with me from day one. We have shared the greatest gifts God could bless us with—all the laughter and fun. Thanks for showing me love and support.

Finally, Amar'e Stoudemire. Man, I reflect back five years ago and remember sitting in my house in Miami praying and thanking God for this new opportunity of being your personal chef. To fast forward over all the amazing years: the fun, the accomplishments, and the rough times, and we always kept God first. To my boss, business partner, friend, brother, I say, Thank you, the sky is the limit!

281

283

287

288

289

290

Universal Conversion Chart

250 °F = 120 °C

275 °F = 135 °C

300 °F = 150 °C

325 °F = 160 °C

350 °F = 180 °C

375 °F = 190 °C

400 °F = 200 °C

425 °F = 220 °C

450 °F = 230 °C

475 °F = 240 °C

500 °F = 260 °C

MEASUREMENT EQUIVALENTS

Measurements should always be level unless directed otherwise.

$\frac{1}{8}$ teaspoon = 0.5 mL

$\frac{1}{4}$ teaspoon = 1 mL

$\frac{1}{2}$ teaspoon = 2 mL

1 teaspoon = 5 mL

1 tablespoon = 3 teaspoons = $\frac{1}{2}$ fluid ounce = 15 mL

2 tablespoons = $\frac{1}{3}$ cup = 1 fluid ounce = 30 mL

4 tablespoons = $\frac{1}{4}$ cup = 2 fluid ounces = 60 mL

$5\frac{1}{3}$ tablespoons = $\frac{1}{3}$ cup = 3 fluid ounces = 80 mL

8 tablespoons = $\frac{1}{2}$ cup = 4 fluid ounces = 120 mL

$10\frac{2}{3}$ tablespoons = $\frac{2}{3}$ cup = 5 fluid ounces = 160 mL

12 tablespoons = $\frac{3}{4}$ cup = 6 fluid ounces = 180 mL

16 tablespoons = 1 cup = 8 fluid ounces = 240 mL

291